Building the Social Union

Building the Social Union: Perspectives, Directions and Challenges

Edited by
Tom McIntosh

Canadian Plains Research Center
University of Regina
2002

Saskatchewan Insitute of Public Policy
University of Regina
Regina, Saskatchewan S4S 0A2
Canada
Tel: (306) 585-5777
Fax: (306) 585-5780

National Library of Canada Cataloguing in Publication Data

Main entry under title:
Building the social union

(Saskatchewan Institute of Public Policy publications, ISSN 1499-6693 ; 1)
Co-published by: Saskatchewan Institute of Public Policy.
Includes bibliographical references and index.
ISBN 0-88977-133-2

1. Canada–Social policy. 2. Federal-provincial relations–Canada.
3. Saskatchewan–Social policy. I. McIntosh, Thomas A. (Thomas Allan),
1964- II. Saskatchewan Institute of Public Policy.   III. Series.
HV108.B74 2002   353.5'0971   C2001-911721-3

Cover design: Brian Danchuk Design, Regina

Printed and bound in Canada by
Houghton Boston, Saskatoon
Printed on acid free paper

— Contents —

Acknowledgements

All but one of the papers collected here were first presented at a conference hosted by the Saskatchewan Institute of Public Policy in February of 2000. On behalf of SIPP, I would like to thank our conference partners, the Institute for Research on Public Policy, the School of Policy Studies and the Institute of Intergovernmental Relations at Queen's University, the University of Regina, the University of Saskatchewan and the Community-University Institute for Social Research at the University of Saskatchewan, for their support and their contributions to making the conference a success.

I also want to thank the IRPP and Policy Options for their agreement to publish shorter versions of some of these papers and those of other conference participants in both the April and May 2000 issues of the magazine. An earlier version of Alain Noël's chapter was also issued by the IRPP as a Working Paper in the summer of 2000.

The authors deserve much thanks for their patience during what was a prolonged search for a publisher. This volume is the first to be issued under the auspices of the Canadian Plains Research Center's publishing arrangement with SIPP and I want to thank Brian Mlazgar and David Gauthier both for their agreement to have CPRC act as SIPP's publisher, but also for the work they did on bringing this particular volume to fruition.

On a personal note, I have been fortunate to call SIPP my academic home since the fall of 1999. In July of 2001 I joined the staff of the Romanow Commission on Health Care and will take a teaching position at the University of Windsor in 2002. I want to take this opportunity to thank my SIPP colleagues, both past (Duane Adams, Katherine Fafard and Ian Rongve) and present (Raymond Blake, John Allan, Erna Pearson, Kathryn Curran, Howard Leeson and Greg Marchildon) for their support and camaraderie over the past few years. It has been a pleasure to watch and participate in the growth of an organization that has accomplished a great deal in its first few years and which I am sure will continue to contribute to the public policy debates facing both Saskatchewan and the country in the coming years.

Tom McIntosh
Regina, SK
May 2001

Contributors

HERMAN BAKVIS is Professor of Political Science at Dalhousie University in Halifax, Nova Scotia

GERARD W. BOYCHUK is Assistant Professor of Political Science at the University of Waterloo in Waterloo, Ontario

DAVID M. CAMERON is Professor of Political Science at Dalhousie University in Halifax, Nova Scotia

TOM MCINTOSH was the Senior Policy Analyst at the Saskatchewan Institute of Public Policy and is currently Assistant Professor of Political Science at the University of Windsor in Windsor, Ontario

JOHN MCLEAN teaches in the Department of Political Studies at Queen's University in Kingston, Ontario

MATTHEW MENDELSOHN is Associate Professor of Political Studies at Queen's University in Kingston, Ontario

ALAIN NOËL is Associate Professor of Political Science at the Université de Montreal in Montreal, Quebec

MICHAEL J. PRINCE is Lansdowne Professor of Social Policy and Associate Dean of the Faculty of Human and Social Development at the University of Victoria in Victoria, British Columbia

CHAPTER ONE

As Time Goes By: Building on SUFA's Commitments[1]

Tom McIntosh

In February 2002 the Social Union Framework Agreement (SUFA) will reach its third anniversary and the governments of Canada will decide whether, as set out in the agreement, they are going to renew the commitments contained in the document. In the period since February 1999 when the federal government and nine provincial governments signed the agreement, a number of things have changed. The Canadian economy, while perhaps not in recession, has slowed down considerably. The federal Liberal party has secured its third successive majority government, defying most predictions that it not only would lose seats, but that it could well slip to minority status. Quebec premier Lucien Bouchard has resigned and been replaced by Finance Minister Bernard Landry, widely presumed to be more of a hardline sovereignist than his predecessor. British Columbia, Saskatchewan, Manitoba, Nova Scotia, Prince Edward Island and Newfoundland all have new leaders and/or new governments as well.

Some things, of course, have not changed. Quebec, which refused to sign the SUFA in the first instance, remains officially opposed to the kind of "collaborative federalism" embodied by the agreement. The health of Canada's publicly administered health care system remains the prime social policy concern of Canadians and is now the subject of an eighteen-month inquiry headed by former Saskatchewan premier Roy Romanow. This despite the fact that an agreement reached between Ottawa and all the provinces saw the federal government partially restore the cuts to provincial transfers following the introduction of the Canada Health and Social Transfer (CHST). And, perhaps most importantly, the concept of a "social union" remains an issue of debate, controversy and interest to only a small number of academics, government policy analysts and commentators.

The intent of this chapter is to provide some contextual analysis for the chapters that follow. The first section provides a brief historical overview of the political processes that led to the signing of the SUFA in 1999. The second section provides an overview of the contents of the document itself. The final section examines both the impact that the agreement has had to date and, in reference to the chapters that follow, the challenges that remain to be faced as the agreement comes up for renewal in 2002.

From "Social Union" to SUFA

In the first instance, there is no shared definition of what is encompassed by the term

---

1. The author would like to thank Vikkram Singh for his research assistance in the preparation of this chapter.

"social union." In her influential monograph prepared for the Canadian Policy Research Networks, Margaret Biggs referred to the social union as the

> web of rights and obligations between Canadian citizens and governments that give effect and meaning to our shared sense of social purpose and common citizenship. The social union embodies our sense of collective responsibility (among citizens), our federalism pact (between and across regions) and our governance contract (between citizens and governments).[2]

Biggs herself points out, though, that as far back as 1994, the Speech from the Throne spoke of a "Charter of Social Security for the whole of Canada" that would commit the federal government to "a grand design … that would articulate the nation's aspirations."[3]

The Pepin-Robarts Commission in 1979 called for the establishment of instruments to increase co-operation within the social and political union to prevent unilateral federal actions and reduce the intergovernmental tension arising from the increased fiscal burden associated with shared-cost social programs. In 1985 the Macdonald Commission proposed federal-provincial-territorial ministerial councils, including a Council of Ministers of Social Policy, as a vehicle for intergovernmental negotiation and consultation to again manage the federal-provincial tensions around the financing and delivery of social programs. Indeed, the term "social union" emerged as a complement and counterweight to the idea of the "economic union" that was the prime focus of the Macdonald Commission's market-oriented recommendations.

The 1992 Charlottetown Accord, aimed at reconciling the province of Quebec to the 1982 constitutional amendments as well as accommodating the demands of other provinces, included a provision that committed Canadian governments to "preserving and developing" Canada's economic and social union. The defeat of the Charlottetown Accord in a national referendum moved the intergovernmental agenda increasingly towards what Harvey Lazar has deemed to be "non-constitutional renewal of the federation." This process was motivated by the federal government's desire to, first, demonstrate to Quebecers that the country was not stuck in status quo federalism (despite the inability to reach agreement on constitutional change), and, second, to inculcate an intergovernmental process that would allow the federal government to get its own fiscal house in order.[4]

Yet the federal government was not the only agent of change. The failure of the Charlottetown Accord in 1992, the election of the federal Liberals in 1993 and the narrow victory of the federalist forces in the 1995 Quebec referendum all combined to focus the attention of many of the provincial governments on the need to find a means of managing the federation that did not involve the high politics of constitutionalism. The background papers originating from the 1996 Annual Premiers Conference (APC) all point towards an increased desire on the part of the provinces to reorient intergovernmental relations in the realm of social policy and included a call "to design options for mechanisms and processes to develop and promote adherence to national principles and standards."[5]

---

2. Margaret Biggs, *Building Blocks for Canada's New Social Union,* Working Paper No. F[02] (Ottawa: Canadian Policy Research Networks, 1996), 1.

3. Ibid., 5.

4. Harvey Lazar, "Non-Constitutional Renewal: Toward a New Equilibrium in the Federation," in Harvey Lazar (ed.), *Non-Constitutional Renewal* (Canada: The State of the Federation, 1997) (Kingston: SPS/McGill-Queen's University Press, 1998), 3–38.

5. Provincial-Territorial Working Group on Social Policy Reform and Renewal, "Issues Paper on Social Policy Reform and Renewal: Next Steps," 13 (prepared for the 37th Annual Premiers Conference, Jasper, Alberta, August 1997).

The premiers' talks on social policy were fuelled in part by the release, just prior to the 1996 APC, of a paper by Queen's University economist Thomas Courchene which had been prepared for the government of Ontario. Entitled "ACCESS: A Convention on the Canadian Economic and Social Systems," the paper proposed a two-stage approach for the development of national standards in the realm of social policy. An interim stage would be characterized by a high level of federal-provincial collaboration designed to insure continuity in social programs while governments tackled their individual fiscal problems. The final stage, termed "the full ACCESS model" by Courchene, would see the provinces take the lead in developing and enforcing national standards and in the creation of new programs. In Courchene's view, the goal was to achieve pan-Canadian goals through "interprovincial collaboration" rather than the more traditional intergovernmentalism that so often relied on unilateral actions taken by the federal government.[6] Whatever one makes of Courchene's fairly radical decentralism, the "ACCESS" paper, along with the work of Margaret Biggs noted above, became the focal points of an increasingly energetic debate both within governments and the academic policy community designed to put flesh on the bones of the idea of (re)creating a Canadian social union.

In August 1998 the attendance of Quebec premier Bouchard at the Premiers Conference in Saskatoon gave a much-needed boost to the social union initiative. For the first time, the provinces were able to present a united front to the federal government, and insofar as "non-constitutional renewal" was, from a federal perspective, aimed at demonstrating to Quebec that "Canada works," then his presence was crucial. The main demands of the provinces related to the commitment on the part of the federal government to let the provinces opt out of any new federally sponsored social program while allowing them to keep the cash earmarked for that new program. The only requirement would be that the monies transferred would be spent on the general area related to the new program. In addition, the provinces asked for joint federal-provincial management of federally sponsored programs, the establishment of an independent dispute-resolution process, and a commitment that the federal government would not introduce any new social programs without the consent of a majority of the provinces.

The good news for Ottawa was that for the first time there was a unanimous recognition that the federal government did have a role in social initiatives even though, constitutionally, such programs tended to fall into provincial jurisdictions. This recognition would, to some extent, cause political problems for Bouchard's relations with the more hard-line sovereignist elements within his government, insofar as it appeared to concede a role to the federal government that many simply did not accept. At the same time, the ability of the provinces to opt out of federal programs with compensation was a key component for Quebec's willingness to continue with the negotiations — negotiations that were interrupted by the Quebec election in late 1998.

The months between December 1998 and the signing of the agreement without the participation of Quebec in February 1999 were marked by multiple proposals, conflicting interpretations around "opting-out with compensation" and renewed demands by the provinces that the federal government restore the cuts to provincial transfers made with the introduction of the CHST in 1995. Ottawa was willing to compensate provinces that opted out of jointly funded social programs, but wanted to reserve the right to not compensate those provinces that refused to participate in new programs fully funded by the federal government.

---

6. Courchene's paper, along with a series of commentaries both critical and supportive, can be found in *Assessing ACCESS: Towards a New Social Union, Proceedings of the Symposium on the Courchene Proposal* (Kingston: Institute of Intergovernmental Relations, 1997).

For the province of Quebec, this was simply not a large enough constraint on the federal government's spending power and would, in its view, continue to allow the federal government to interfere in areas of provincial jurisdiction.

In the end, nine provincial governments were willing to concede to the federal government the right not to compensate those provinces that opted out of new federally funded programs. This was a concession that the government of Quebec was unwilling to make and, though some of its rationale may lie in its sovereignist stance (i.e., that signing any intergovernmental agreement would be a concession that "federalism can be made to work"), it needs to be recognized that this position was also endorsed by the federalist opposition in the Quebec National Assembly. Despite the refusal of Quebec, the SUFA was signed by the federal government and nine provinces in February 1999 along with a side agreement (which Quebec did sign) that provided for an increase in federal transfers to the provinces on the condition that the money be spent on their cash-strapped health systems. The irony in all of this is that in their attempt to demonstrate that governments could renew the federation through non-constitutional agreement, the governments again reached agreement without Quebec.

For some, the absence of Quebec's signature is "the agreement's most serious weakness."[7] For others, the SUFA, while not perfect and in need of further refinement, constitutes a recognition of both the political and policy interdependence of the two orders of government and the need to preserve their autonomy as granted by the constitution.[8] What remains to be seen is whether the SUFA is in fact "a first step" that will followed by others designed to further refine the relationship between governments and between governments and their citizens, or whether the apparent isolation of Quebec becomes a permanent feature of both the constitutional and non-constitutional order of the federation.

What SUFA Says

The Social Union Framework Agreement exists as an administrative agreement between the federal government and nine provinces — it has no legal or justiciable force and its authority rests entirely on the political will of its signatories to live up to its terms. As Lazar has argued:

> the Framework Agreement could turn out to be a major innovation in the workings of the federation, heralding a new era of collaboration, mutual respect among the orders of government and a more coherent and systematic approach to social policy making… Alternately, it could be ignored by its signatories and relegated to a footnote in the country's history.[9]

Contrary to what one might think at first blush, the SUFA is not an agreement about "the nuts and bolts" of social policy or specific social programs. Rather, it is focussed primarily on the governance of social policy — and especially on the intergovernmental aspects of that governance — and attempts to provide a framework that would balance both interdependence and independence while strengthening the accountability of governments not to each other but to their respective citizenries. Indeed, it may be the agreement's commitments to increasing government-to-citizen accountability, transparency and engagement that are among its most important elements.

---

7. Alain-G. Gagnon and Hugh Segal, "Introduction," *The Canadian Social Union without Quebec: Eight Critical Analyses* (Montreal: IRPP, 2000), 1.

8. Gregory P. Marchildon, "A Step In the Right Direction," *Inroads* 9 (2000): 124–33.

9. Harvey Lazar, "The Social Union Framework Agreement and the Future of Fiscal Federalism," in Harvey Lazar (ed.), *Towards a New Mission Statement for Canadian Fiscal Federalism* (Canada: The State of the Federation, 1999/2000) (Kingston: SPS/McGill-Queen's University Press, 2000), 100.

The agreement, reprinted in full in the Appendix to this volume, contains commitments in seven areas, some of which can be seen to be about "process" and some of which might be more properly seen to be about "substance." However, as Lazar again notes, such a clear distinction between substance and process, while useful for academic discussions of public administration, is of less use in the real world of intergovernmental negotiation and policy-making. The terms of the agreement, however, can be outlined in the following manner:

- An introductory section relating to fundamental Canadian values such as equality, diversity, fairness, individual dignity and responsibility and mutual respect;

- Commitments to strengthening pan-Canadian mobility by not erecting new barriers to mobility in new social program initiatives and to a process for eliminating (within three years) existing barriers to mobility that might inhibit access to health services, post-secondary education, training, employment and other social services;

- Commitments to increase transparency, accountability and clarity on the part of governments and to provide Canadians with a greater voice in monitoring and measuring the outcomes and performance of social programs while also insuring the active participation of Canadians in developing and evaluating social policy initiatives;

- Commitments to a new approach to the use of the federal spending power[10] to insure funding predictability, increased cooperation between governments on common goals and to insure provincial and territorial flexibility in the design and delivery of social programs adapted to local needs and circumstances;

- Commitments to providing advance notice to other governments before implementing a major change in specific social programs that would effect other governments; to consult prior to such implementation, and to promote joint actions by sharing information on emerging social trends, priorities and problems;

- Guidelines for the avoidance of intergovernmental disputes and for the resolution of such disputes as do arise, beginning with a joint fact-finding report and the use of third-party mediation;

- Provisions for a public review of the agreement within three years.

As noted above, the overall purpose of the SUFA is not to deal with the specific problems evident in particular social policy sectors — underfunding of the health system, poverty, declining Employment Insurance coverage or the federal role in post-secondary education — but is about both how governments will relate to each other and to their citizens when (and if) they attempt to redesign specific programs. In short, the agreement is mostly about how future social policy initiatives will be undertaken rather than about the content of specific programs and policies.

To many of its critics, the SUFA fails precisely because it is about "how to make social policy" rather than being about "the content of social policy." For example, Shelagh Day, Special Advisor on Human Rights to the National Association of Women and the Law, called the agreement "a social union framework for governments, not for people" and lamented its

---

10. As in most federations, the federal government in Canada has the right to spend money in virtually any area that it sees fit regardless of whether a particular area is a matter of federal or provincial jurisdiction. While the Canadian courts have recognized this right, its exercise by the federal government has long been a source of intergovernmental tension and the restriction of the federal spending power has been demanded not only by Quebec but by many of the provinces which have seen it as a means of federal interference with provincial social policy and fiscal priorities. For an overview of how the spending power is used in different federations, including Canada, see Ronald L. Watts, *The Spending Power in Federal Systems: A Comparative Study* (Kingston: Institute of Intergovernmental Relations, 1999).

unenforceable status.[11] Bruce Porter, of the Charter Committee on Poverty Issues, called the agreement "empty of promise for the lives of citizens."[12]

These critics are, in part, correct in their analysis. But they are criticizing the agreement for not being something that it was never intended to be. They are correct in their assertion that the (re)creation of a stronger social union requires a set of programs that meets the needs of citizens in a more comprehensive and productive manner and which insures that services are available when and where individuals need them. But the design and provision of those services are the responsibility of the individual governments in Canada, working either collaboratively or independently as appropriate, and can not be achieved through an administrative agreement such as the SUFA. All that the SUFA can do is provide a set of principles and objectives that can guide the future development of social policy initiatives.

Numerous organizations, including those noted above and the nationalist Council of Canadians, further criticized the SUFA for failing to set out enforceable "national standards" for social policy. Almost certainly, the phrase "national standards" is meant to refer to the supposed national standards included in the Canada Health Act (CHA). The CHA provides that the federal government will provide funds for provincial health systems only insofar as the provinces commit themselves to a health system that is "publicly administered," "comprehensive," "portable," "universal," and "accessible." As important as these principles are for the preservation of the public-funded health systems in the country, they in no way constitute "national standards" and, with the exception of the prohibition of so-called "extra-billing," have never been treated as national standards by the federal government. For example, the commitment to a "comprehensive" health system is undefined except that in includes "medically necessary" procedures delivered in hospitals and doctors' offices. It is left to the province to decide what services are medically necessary and what services will or will not be insured under a provincial health system.

Furthermore, no one can seriously claim that a country with such a small population spread over such a wide geographic area and with limited fiscal resources could provide the same accessibility to health services for all its citizens regardless of location. If rural residents must travel (sometimes significant distances) to receive certain specialized health services while residents of large urban centres have access to such services in their own locality, is the "standard" of accessibility being violated? Does a province the size of Prince Edward Island, with 100,000 residents, violate the CHA if it chooses to send residents needing specific and very specialized services out of province because it is fiscally imprudent to try to support such an infrastructure locally? It makes more sense to assume that the principles of the CHA are just that — principles — and that they can only serve as guidelines for the reasonable provision of a reasonable level of services at a reasonable cost to the public purse. Furthermore, the adherence to those principles by governments (and the definition of what is reasonable in specific circumstances) is best enforced politically by a citizenry that values and wishes to protect the publicly funded health system.

What is even more disturbing about some of social policy advocates' criticisms of the SUFA is the underlying assumption that only the federal government can enforce standards of service delivery around social policy. This flies in the face of the fact that it was federal unilateral action that created the CHST and saw transfers to the provinces fall dramatically in the 1990s — one of the very acts that prompted the need for an agreement like the SUFA

---

11. "Social Union Framework Heartless Say Social Union Justice Groups" (Social union press release and Backgrounder) at: http://www.povnet.wen.net/socialunion.html

12. Ibid.

to reestablish a set of rules around the distribution of fiscal resources for social policy.[13] Within its own realm, the federal government's reform of the Unemployment Insurance system into Employment Insurance resulted in massive decreases of coverage for unemployed Canadians, the effects of which may become increasingly stark if the country enters a recession in the near future.[14]

This is not to suggest that provincial governments were themselves angels in the realm of social policy restructuring over the past decade, as the many cuts to social assistance provision and eligibility demonstrate so ably. Rather, it is to suggest that no one order of government has any greater or lesser commitment to a comprehensive, progressive and sustainable social union. It is true that individual governments may have greater or lesser commitments to specific kinds of social policy and may be more or less willing to consider specific policy options. But that is how it has always been. Medicare in its initial incarnation was a provincial program brought about because one province was willing to take the political risk of introducing public health insurance. (It is worth noting that one of the oft-forgotten consequences of Saskatchewan's introduction of Medicare and the strike by doctors that followed was that CCF premier Woodrow Lloyd lost the subsequent provincial election.)

All this is to say that any serious (re)creation of a social union is, fundamentally, a political process that will necessitate not only a commitment on the part of governments to accept a new set of intergovernmental rules, but will require that the public be both able and willing to hold their governments to account for the actions they take on specific social policy priorities. While it is true that the SUFA is, to a great degree, the creation of the kind of executive federalism so much decried in the aftermath of the Meech Lake and Charlottetown Accords, it should be recognized that the signatory governments have, within the SUFA, made new commitments about accountability to their citizenries and to the transparency of the policy process.

It may be relatively easy to dismiss these commitments as so much window-dressing designed to deflect criticisms of decisions taken by "eleven men behind closed doors" (or ten in this specific case). But having made the commitment to engage citizens in a more deliberative manner and to develop the means to report to citizens on program outcomes in a more transparent manner, the governments should at least be given the opportunity to demonstrate their willingness to live up to those commitments. Those sections of the agreement dealing with the development of new means of designing and reporting on social policy should be neither dismissed out of hand nor taken at face value. If taken seriously by both governments and citizens they could provide an important step in pulling citizens into policy processes from which they have all too often been excluded and in inculcating a different bureaucratic culture on the part of government policy makers. It is unfair to dismiss those parts of the agreement as "meaningless"[15] until such time as both government and citizens have been given the opportunity to imbue them with some meaning. Three years may be too short a time to initiate such a far-reaching change in the way policy is developed and implemented, but

---

13. Harvey Lazar, "The Federal Role in the New Social Union: Ottawa at a Crossroads," in *Non-Constitutional Renewal*, 105–36.

14. Tom McIntosh and Gerard W. Boychuk, "Dis-Covered: Social Assistance, Employment Insurance and the Growing Gap in Income Support for Unemployed Canadians," in Tom McIntosh (ed.), *Federalism, Democracy and Labour Market Policy in Canada* (Kingston: SPS/McGill-Queen's University Press, 2000), 65–158; and Gerard W. Boychuk and Tom McIntosh, "Adrift Between the Islands: Employment Insurance, Social Assistance and the Politics of Income Support in Canada," *Canadian Review of Social Policy* (spring 2001).

15. Council of Canadians, "Social Union Could Pull Provinces Into a Race to the Bottom, Warns Council of Canadians," Campaigns, http://www.canadians.org/campaign/campaigns-socialmedia02.html

governments will likely be judged harshly when the time comes to renew the SUFA if there is no demonstrable progress on these specific commitments.

As a document the SUFA is far from perfect. Some of its language is vague, but that is the nature of such agreements. The debate between what the agreement says and what it means will continue to play itself out as part of an ongoing iterative process. As with the Charter of Rights and Freedoms, its meaning may well change and evolve over time. If it survives long enough to be renewed, it may also survive long enough to be amended, clarified, expanded or shortened.

Beyond the vagueness of some of the language, the agreement has some deficiencies in content as well. Having weathered the federal government's unilateral reduction in funding following the introduction of the CHST, the provinces are rightly concerned about the use of the federal spending power in times of economic growth. The provinces' concern, especially in Quebec, that the federal government could first create and then withdraw from new social programs that would leave them responsible for the financing should not be dismissed lightly. Indeed, if Quebec is going to be a signatory to any future revised version of the SUFA then the federal government is going to have to accept that it will have to constrain its urge to move into politically popular areas of provincial jurisdiction when it is flush with cash. That means that more explicit restrictions may need to be put on the federal spending power.

Equally important, the governments who signed the agreement are going to have to demonstrate that it has begun a process of policy-making that is both more accountable and more transparent. For example, the September 2000 intergovernmental agreement on health care financing, which saw the partial restoration of federal transfers to the pre-CHST levels, was a debate almost entirely played out in terms of dollars — who had them, how many they had and who wanted them. Important concerns about how effectively current expenditures are being spent, about primary care reform, the role of technological innovation as a cost-driver within the system, the cost of pharmaceuticals and the relationship between health spending and spending on those other areas that are themselves determinants of a population's health (e.g. education, labour market policy, etc.) were lost in the intergovernmental wrangling over money. Unless some demonstrable progress is made in governments being able to assure Canadians that the social union is getting stronger in terms of both its effectiveness and efficiency, it may not matter if the agreement is not renewed in 2002.

Perhaps the most important test of the SUFA and the willingness of the governments to live up to the commitments made in it will come with the next economic downturn. If the economy begins to shrink and unemployment begins to rise, then the pressure on social programs will increase. This more than any other development will illustrate whether the SUFA's commitments towards a new kind of intergovernmentalism and a new kind of government-citizen relationship have any lasting impact on the Canadian social union.

Perspectives, Directions and Challenges

The chapters that follow began as presentations to a conference entitled "The Social Union Framework Agreement: Perspectives and Directions," hosted by the Saskatchewan Institute of Public Policy (SIPP) and co-sponsored by the Institute for Research on Public Policy (IRPP) in Regina in February 2000. A number of the presentations, including some by the authors collected here, were later published in abbreviated form by the IRPP's journal *Policy Options* in the May and June 2000 issues. The purpose of this collection is to present more detailed and sustained analyses of what the SUFA accomplished, what it failed to accomplish, and what work remains to be done if the agreement is to become a vital component of Canada's social union. What is quite evident is that each of the authors views the strengths, weaknesses, accomplishments and challenges facing the (re)creation of the social union through very different lenses.

Broadly speaking, the papers can be divided into two types. In the first instance, this chapter as well as those by Noël and Mendelsohn and McLean focus on the SUFA itself and its place in Canada's intergovernmental universe. By contrast, the chapters by Boychuk, McIntosh, Bakvis and Cameron and Prince focus on specific policy areas or challenges and, as such, seek to understand what the SUFA may or may not mean for each of those policy areas.

Alain Noël has, in recent years, distinguished himself as one of the most eloquent critics not only of the specific content of the SUFA, but also of the kind of intergovernmentalism that spawned the agreement. Noël's chapter calls into question the nature and extent of the "collaboration" that supposedly characterizes this new era of non-constitutional renewal of the federation. Drawing a parallel between the rise of "new public management" approaches to public administration within the federal civil service, Noël characterizes the "collaboration" between the federal government and the provinces in the SUFA negotiations as a case of the federal government still playing the role of the senior partner — the group that "steers" while the provinces are forced to "row."

Noël goes on to criticize the very notion that the SUFA can be considered a collaborative document given the absence of Quebec's signature. For collaboration to occur, he argues, the process must be non-hierarchical and truly accommodating of differences in approach. But the willingness of the federal government and the other provinces to proceed without Quebec demonstrates not a willingness to accept administrative asymmetry in the federation, but rather a hierarchical approach to intergovernmentalism that he labels "hegemonic cooperation" in which Ottawa still calls the shots. Thus, the SUFA represents a potentially pathological development in Canadian federalism whereby Quebec will find itself increasingly isolated from the other provinces.

Mendelsohn and McLean focus their attention on an aspect of the SUFA that is often overlooked in favour of a concentration on its intergovernmental aspects. As noted above, the SUFA is not just (or even primarily) about government-to-government relations, but also about government-to-citizen relations. The SUFA's commitment to increased reporting to citizens on social policy outcomes and the development of a more transparent policy process are designed to yield higher levels of accountability of governments to citizens. Taking this even further, the agreement explicitly commits the governments to designing and implementing new means by which citizens can participate in the policy process at various stages.

The authors, taking the governments at their word, outline a series of recommendations that are designed to make real the commitments to "engage citizens" in the (re)design of the Canadian social union. Most importantly, the authors provide a compelling argument on the necessity of such engagement. The bureaucratic tendency to try to tightly control the policy process can, they argue, result in governments effectively losing control of a process that is undermined by a cynical public which has been pushed out of the process. Engaging citizens and providing a forum where competing interests must reach compromises through deliberative processes can not only serve to reconnect citizens to their governments but can also result in policies that may more fully meet the needs of those citizens. The authors are fully aware of the challenges of altering the traditional way of policy development and implementation and there are no illusions about the difficulties that are likely to be encountered as governments attempt new kinds of engagement. In the final analysis, however, Mendelsohn and McLean argue governments are going to have to loosen their grip on policy formation if they truly want to hold onto it.

The four remaining papers focus less on the intergovernmental aspects of the agreement or its specific terms and concentrate instead on the building of the social union itself. As such, they deal with specific social policy areas: social assistance, labour market policy, post-secondary education and Aboriginal policy.

For his part, Gerard Boychuk is unconvinced that either the SUFA or the process of inter-governmentalism it engenders will yield much in terms of better provincial social assistance policies. Using the National Child Benefit as an example, Boychuk argues that it is less than clear that anything substantial has been done to affect the lives of children in poverty and that collaboration for collaboration's sake does not necessarily yield better social policy. Boychuk reminds us that there are real policy differences being debated in the area of social assistance policy and that federal-provincial wrangling is not just politicians bickering over jurisdiction, but rather the articulation of very different policy priorities. Thus, to the extent that "collaboration" takes priority over the actual content of social policy, then one should not be surprised that social policy suffers.

McIntosh's examination of the role of labour market policy in the social union is also somewhat pessimistic, but for different reasons. In the first instance, he is critical of the lack of attention that has been paid to labour market policy — both in terms of active and pas-sive measures — within the context of the social union debates. At the same time, he notes, the sector has undergone some significant changes with the devolution of active measures to the provinces, the reform of UI into EI and provincial restructuring of social assistance pro-vision. All of this has been accomplished, he argues, with little regard to how the various ele-ments of labour market policy interact with each other or how these changes will withstand an economic downturn. In the event of a recession, more pressure will be put on both income support and retraining programs, and their failure to deliver adequate protection to Canadians in need may well usher in a period of intergovernmental finger-pointing that will quickly dissipate the goodwill of collaboration.

If labour market policy proper has been more or less ignored in the social union debates, then post-secondary education (PSE) is the other sector living in obscurity. As Cameron and Bakvis make clear, there is no real consensus on how or whether PSE fits into either the social union or the SUFA itself. Though PSE is clearly a provincial responsibility, the feder-al government has a long history as a supporter of academic scholarship and research (e.g. through the Social Sciences and Humanities Research Council, the Natural Sciences and Engineering Research Council and the new Canadian Institutes for Health Research that replaced the Medical Research Council) and of students through the federal student loan program.

But as the authors clearly demonstrate, the federal role in PSE is much more than those most visible elements and the history of federal influence in the sector has tended to wax and wane over the decades. Since the 1970s the federal government withdrew from direct sup-port for PSE and focussed on labour market development policy and the cuts to the provin-cial transfers in the mid-1990s seemed to indicate that the CHST was on its way to becom-ing only a "health and welfare" transfer. However, as the federal government devolved much of active labour market policy to the provinces under the Labour Market Development Agreements (LMDAs), it also began to increase funding for university-based research and development. Interestingly, for the authors, these developments seem to have brought the federal role in PSE back to what it was in the 1960s though in somewhat different form. Thus, the federal government has made PSE an important component of its vision of the Canadian social union, but it seems to have managed to recreate its role in the sector out-side of the context of the SUFA.

If labour market and post-secondary education policy seem to exist "below the radar" of the SUFA, then it is probably fair to assert that Aboriginal policy was really no more than an afterthought in the process that created the agreement. In his chapter, Michael Prince traces not only the events that led to the signing of the SUFA, but also the manner in which national Aboriginal political organizations (which have grown and matured over the past decades) were effectively marginalized from those intergovernmental processes. But what is most compelling in Prince's analysis is that despite their exclusion from the process that created the SUFA, national Aboriginal political organizations may have some success in influencing the nature and shape of the policy changes that come out of the SUFA as they have an impact on Aboriginal policy.

Though Prince is well aware that the inclusion of national Aboriginal political organizations in the social policy processes of both provincial and federal governments is far from complete, there is some evidence to suggest that these same organizations are beginning to have an effect on how the SUFA is being implemented. In small but meaningful ways, these organizations are having some success in changing the intergovernmental relations and processes that govern social policy affecting Aboriginal peoples and bringing an Aboriginal perspective to the policy development process. While there are still immense challenges and the successes to date have been relatively small, Prince finds some reasons for optimism in the manner by which Aboriginal organizations are making themselves heard in the post-SUFA policy environment.

It is evident that there is certainly no consensus amongst the authors presented here on either the appropriateness of the SUFA or on its potential impact on the nuts and bolts of social policy development. It is also not clear whether the political will exists amongst the signatories of the SUFA to renew the document when it "expires" on its third anniversary. Indeed, it may be fair to say that there is more ambivalence towards the agreement amongst governments now than at any time in the years since its adoption. But it may not matter whether the SUFA is renewed or not because in and of itself it may not be essential to the (re)creation of the social union.

In the same manner that the Canadian economic union is not a product of the Agreement on Internal Trade, but is instead the creation of a host of social and economic forces that rest on the will of citizens and governments to create and sustain a viable nation, so the shape and nature of the social union will ultimately depend not on an administrative agreement but on the commitment of Canadians and their governments to use social policy as a means of reinforcing and strengthening the connections between citizens and between citizens and their governments.

As many of the authors presented here contend, the terms of the SUFA are ultimately much less important than the content of actual social policies that either do or do not provide real services to real citizens in a manner that meets their various needs. Agreements like the SUFA can provide guidance about how policy is created and the principles that can and should guide it, but such agreements are neither inherently necessary for good social policy development and implementation nor are they sufficient for meeting the social policy needs of citizens. Thus, if governments fail to renew the SUFA it may not really change the social policy landscape in Canada in any profound manner. It matters less that there is an agreement signed by governments committing themselves to better and more transparent social policy development than it does that citizens, governments and policy analysts continue the debates about the future direction of social policy that the SUFA has brought to light.

CHAPTER TWO

Without Quebec: Collaborative Federalism with a Footnote?[1]

Alain Noël

Our federation is evolving toward greater cooperation and consensus-building, while respecting the constitutional jurisdictions of each order of government, rather than toward extensive centralization in favour of the federal government or extensive decentralization in favour of the provincial governments.

Stéphane Dion, President of the Queen's Privy Council for Canada
and Minister of Intergovernmental Affairs, April 22, 1999[2]

While sharing essentially the same concerns, the Government of Quebec does not intend to adhere to the federal/provincial/territorial approach to social policies. Furthermore, Quebec did not sign the Social Union Framework Agreement. Consequently, any reference to joint federal/provincial/territorial positions or provincial/territorial positions in this document do not include the Government of Quebec.

Preliminary footnote, in the *Progress Report to Premiers* of the Provincial/Territorial
Council on Social Policy Renewal, August 1999[3]

Canadian federalism is increasingly described as collaborative, to account for what is perceived as a remarkable expansion of non-hierarchical intergovernmental collaboration on a variety of issues ranging from internal trade to child benefits. Until recently, this new brand of federalism was more an outcome than an objective, more the unplanned and mixed result of various pragmatic arrangements than the product of a clear design for the federation. The February 4, 1999, Social Union Framework Agreement (SUFA) changed

---

1. An earlier version of this chapter was published, under the same title, in the Institute for Research on Public Policy's *Policy Matters* series (vol. 1, no. 2, March 2000). I am grateful to Raymond B. Blake and Hugh Segal for their invitation to the Saskatchewan Institute of Public Policy Forum on the Social Union, and to the Forum participants for their helpful comments. I thank, in particular, Keith Banting, David Cameron, Jane Jenson, Harvey Lazar, Tom McIntosh, Denis Saint-Martin, and Richard Simeon for their specific comments and suggestions.

2. Stéphane Dion, "Collaborative Federalism in an Era of Globalization," 1 (Notes for an Address to the Institute of Public Administration of Canada, Ottawa, Department of Intergovernmental Affairs, April 22, 1999).

3. Provincial/Territorial Council on Social Policy Renewal, *Progress Report to Premiers*, 1 (Report No. 4, Québec, August 1999).

this situation fundamentally. For the first time, a broad agreement codified the new rules that would govern intergovernmental relations, in all areas of social policy but also, by extension, in a number of sectors not considered in the document.

The Quebec government was not part of this agreement. The new rules nevertheless apply to Quebec, and the collaborative process goes on as if, or almost as if, all agreed. Shared visions, agreements, agendas, objectives, consultations, outcome indicators, and progress reports regularly come out, usually with a footnote stating that the Government of Quebec shares "essentially the same concerns" but "does not intend to adhere to the federal-provincial-territorial approach" and is not included in the analysis or in the stated positions.

Most observers have portrayed this situation as less than ideal, but nevertheless satisfactory in the circumstances. Some have even suggested that the outcome is helpful because it creates *de facto* asymmetry in Canadian federalism. I wish to argue, on the contrary, that collaborative federalism with a footnote is the worst possible outcome of a process that was not well engaged and did not require such a rapid and superficial conclusion. The SUFA is detrimental because it is not a truly collaborative achievement, because it is not faithful to the federal principle and to Canadian tradition, and because it does not augur well for social policy in Canada.

This chapter discusses these arguments in three parts. The first argues that for collaboration to be non-hierarchical, it must produce cooperative solutions when there are significant differences in interests and perceptions. The social union negotiations constituted a good test in this respect, and their abrupt conclusion, defined and paid for by the federal government, fits oddly with the idea of non-hierarchical collaboration. It corresponds well, however, to an understanding of Canadian federalism as hegemonic cooperation, driven by the logic of what Donald Savoie has called court government. The second part addresses the question of asymmetry, to explain that the failure to include Quebec in the social union and the limited recognition given to the idea of shared sovereignty make the SUFA somewhat asymmetric, but not very federal. Finally, the last part discusses the implications of the new institutional framework for social policy. Collaborative federalism with a footnote will make some policy choices easier than others, and it is likely to produce social policies defined more around persons and through income taxes than around places and through services. If there is such a thing as a "Third Way," the Canadian version will bear the imprint of the federal Department of Finance.

Non-Hierarchical Collaboration?

Peut-être que j'hallucine
Peut-être que quelqu'un a mis dans mon gin
Deux trois kilos de narcotine
Si c'est pas le paradis
L'illusion est exquise
Dieu faites que jamais je ne dégrise
Le monde est rendu peace
Hey qu'on se le dise
Le monde est rendu peace

    Marc Déry, *Le monde est rendu peace*, 1999

The idea of collaborative federalism was coined to characterize the evolution of intergovernmental relations in the second half of the 1990s. When it came to power in 1993, Jean Chrétien's Liberal government turned the page on years of failed attempts at constitutional reform, to concentrate instead on jobs and "good government." The close results of the 1995 Quebec referendum demonstrated the limits of this approach and convinced the federal government to seek "the renewal of the federation through non-constitutional means."[4] The approach was not entirely new, but it became more explicit and ambitious, and involved the different governments in a range of discussions that was unprecedented in scope and in depth. On a number of issues, going from fiscal and trade to labour market and social policy questions, positions were defined, reports were drafted, meetings were held, and compromises were reached or at least envisioned. Most of these compromises were unspectacular but meaningful responses to concrete problems, and they changed intergovernmental relations in an incremental fashion, even though not always in a clear, well-articulated direction.

An Agreement on Internal Trade was signed in 1994, another on a National Child Benefit System was reached in 1996 without Quebec, and bilateral agreements on active labour market programs were obtained with most provinces (including Quebec), along with a host of arrangements or understandings regarding child wellbeing, health, benefits and services for persons with disabilities, other labour market matters, education, Aboriginal affairs, the status of women, housing, and fiscal issues. Numerous intergovernmental meetings continue to take place, involving various levels of officials and reaching well into specific and technical issues. For an external observer, it is becoming increasingly difficult to keep track of an evolution that is rapid, multifaceted and fine grained. Progress reports list a variety of minute achievements that do not add up easily into a coherent or meaningful whole. In many instances, the progress seems to lie more in the process than in tangible policy consequences.

The concept of collaborative federalism was introduced to make sense of this evolution. Harvey Lazar, who has produced the best analyses on this question, contrasts collaborative federalism with earlier forms of cooperative and executive federalism in Canada. Whereas the cooperative and executive federalism of the previous decades saw the different governments manage interdependence within a basically hierarchical framework, the collaborative federalism of the late 1990s would entail a joint management of interdependence embodying "a greater respect for the idea that the two orders of government should relate to one another on a *non-hierarchical* basis."[5] Lazar's formulation — "a greater respect for the idea" — acknowledges that, in many ways, Canadian federalism remains hierarchical. The collaborative model is a project in the making, more advanced in some policy sectors than in others, and not fully accepted, even in Ottawa. Still, argues Lazar, overall the federal approach "is becoming more collaborative."[6]

As with cooperative or executive federalism, the concept of collaborative federalism does not need to apply to all intergovernmental processes or arrangements. It is used to characterize a period, to describe a series of trends and evolutions that together set the tone for intergovernmental relations. In this respect, the federal approach is indeed "becoming more collaborative." In its November 1999 report, the Auditor General of Canada documents a significant increase in various forms of collaborative arrangements initiated by the federal government. Some of these arrangements involve private partners and are not intergovernmental, but many concern some or all the provinces, often on important policy issues.[7]

---

4. Harvey Lazar, "Non-Constitutional Renewal: Toward a New Equilibrium in the Federation," in Harvey Lazar (ed.), *Canada: The State of the Federation 1997; Non-Constitutional Renewal* (Kingston: Queen's University, Institute of Intergovernmental Relations, 1998), 7.

5. Italics in the original; ibid., 24.

6. Harvey Lazar, "The Federal Role in a New Social Union: Ottawa at a Crossroads," in Lazar (ed.), *Canada: The State of the Federation 1997*, 131–32.

7. Auditor General of Canada, *Report* (Ottawa: Auditor General of Canada, 1999), 23-10, 23-11.

But what does collaboration mean in this context? Is it equivalent to "cooperation between governments," as Intergovernmental Affairs Minister Stéphane Dion suggests? Does it really deserve to be celebrated as "governance the Canadian way"?[8] Does it provide a good and genuinely new avenue for non-constitutional reform?

At the outset, a note of caution is necessary regarding the looseness of the vocabulary on these questions. In current discussions, collaboration and cooperation are often used interchangeably. The notion of collaborative federalism has also been adopted in the recent past to describe a different situation, namely the high-profile reconciliation and accommodation efforts of the Mulroney government in the middle of the 1980s.[9] As for the cooperative federalism of the 1960s, it could probably be better described as a form of "federal unilateralism."[10] I will work, here, with Harvey Lazar's definition, which associates collaborative federalism with "the idea that the two orders of government should relate to one another on a *non-hierarchical* basis."

To collaborate and to cooperate mean roughly the same thing, namely to work together. If the work is done on a non-hierarchical basis, it implies that decisions are not determined through a chain of command. All partners may not have the same influence on the outcome, but agreements are produced through mutual adjustments and negotiations, rather than through hierarchy.

Collaboration, or cooperation, is always difficult. Even when there is a common interest, working together requires coordination and compromise. When the promotion of a common interest is automatically obtained and does not demand mutual adjustments, coordination or negotiations, there is no need to collaborate. "Harmony," explains Robert Keohane, "is apolitical. No communication is necessary, and no influence need be exercised. Cooperation, by contrast, is highly political: somehow, patterns of behavior must be altered."[11] In other words, cooperation, or collaboration, presupposes conflict. It is the ability to overcome conflict, to work together despite differences in interests or in perceptions, that is the true test of a collaborative arrangement.

This implies that when collaboration matters most, when divergences are significant, it tends to remain imperfect and fragile. In this perspective, the achievements of collaborative federalism may be seen as positive. After all, there are genuine collaborative efforts, some give and take on each side, and tangible institutional results.[12] Collaboration, however, has often emerged in areas where little adjustments were necessary, where in fact it did not mean much. With the more critical National Child Benefit and the SUFA, by contrast, collaboration was mainly obtained because the provinces yielded and because the absence of Quebec at the table was deemed unimportant.

---

8. Dion, "Collaborative Federalism in an Era of Globalization," 6.

9. Richard Simeon and Ian Robinson, *State, Society, and the Development of Canadian Federalism*, Volume 71 of the Studies Prepared for the Royal Commission on the Economic Union and Development Prospects for Canada (Toronto: University of Toronto Press, 1990), 301.

10. Lazar, "The Federal Role in a New Social Union," 110.

11. Robert O. Keohane, *After Hegemony: Cooperation and Discord in the World Political Economy* (Princeton: Princeton University Press, 1984), 53.

12. Such positive assessments are presented in: David Cameron and Richard Simeon, "Intergovernmental Relations and Democratic Citizenship," in B. Guy Peters and Donald J. Savoie (eds.), *Governance in the Twenty-first Century: Revitalizing the Public Service* (Montreal and Kingston: Canadian Centre for Management Development and McGill-Queen's University Press, 2000), 80; Harvey Lazar, "The Social Union Framework Agreement and the Future of Fiscal Federalism," in Harvey Lazar (ed.), *Canada: The State of the Federation 1999/2000; Toward a New Mission Statement for Canadian Fiscal Federalism* (Kingston: Queen's University, Institute of Intergovernmental Relations, 2000), 115; and Thomas J. Courchene, *A State of Minds: Toward a Human Capital Future for Canadians* (Montreal: Institute for Research on Public Policy, 2001), 95, 266.

In Saskatoon, in August 1998, the Quebec government had joined a modified inter-provincial consensus to participate fully in the ongoing federal-provincial discussion on the social union. For the Quebec government, the move was significant. Until then, it had denounced the whole process as "another exercise in pan-Canadianism" that could only undermine Quebec's traditional demands and legitimate the federal government's social policy ambitions. The 1996 agreement on the National Child Benefit, which imposed on Quebec norms and mechanisms defined by the federal government and the provinces, led the Quebec government to define three conditions under which it could join the ongoing discussions on the social union. In Saskatoon, the Quebec government compromised on these three conditions: it left aside unsolved constitutional difficulties to join a bargaining process that did not make the opting-out formula unconditional; it accepted much of the inter-provincial — and pan-Canadian — discourse on the social union; and it recognized implicitly a legitimate role for the federal government in social policy. In exchange, the other provinces agreed to include an opting-out formula in their common position, but only as a bargaining position.[13]

The importance of Quebec's concessions has been underestimated by commentators, both in Quebec and in English Canada. When the provinces turned around to accept, very rapidly, a framework that represented even less than their own, long-held, pre-Saskatoon position, most concluded that the Quebec government was responsible because it never intended to reach an agreement. The fact that real concessions had already been made was not recognized. The fact, as well, that the provinces did not even come close to their own demands did not seem important.

From the point of view of the federal government, the outcome made sense. The SUFA that was adopted was basically the one federal civil servants had written, borrowing the inter-provincial vocabulary but conceding little that had not already been offered. The lack of support in Quebec, even from the federalist official opposition, which did not approve the SUFA, apparently did not matter.

For the provinces, the result seemed more problematic, since the SUFA did not retain much from years of efforts to circumscribe the use of the federal spending power and redefine intergovernmental relations.[14] Even if we ignore Quebec's concerns, the terms of the SUFA seem quite distant from the provinces' initial demands. Before Quebec joined the provincial common front, the premiers had already advanced articulate and relatively ambitious demands to rebalance the federation. They wanted the federal government to accept a reference framework that would be faithful to a certain number of values, would respect the division of powers, and would ensure the stability, predictability and flexibility of Canadian social policies. Some of these objectives are found, in more or less modified forms, in the SUFA. This is notably the case with the most general pan-Canadian principles such as equality, access to services, respect for the structure of health care services, and the idea of sufficient and durable financing. The most important objectives from the provincial viewpoint, however, were cast aside or interpreted in a minimalist fashion. The SUFA leaves the provinces in a subordinate role, imposes stricter mobility rules, does not integrate a strong and credible federal commitment to sufficient, stable and predictable

13. Alain Noël, "General Study of the Framework Agreement," in Alain G. Gagnon and Hugh Segal (eds.), *The Canadian Social Union without Quebec: Eight Critical Analyses* (Montreal: Quebec Studies Program of McGill University and Institute for Research on Public Policy, 2000), 22–23.

14. William B.P. Robson and Daniel Schwanen, "The Social Union Agreement: Too Flawed to Last," *C.D. Howe Institute Backgrounder* (Toronto: C.D. Howe Institute, February 8, 1999), 3.

funding, creates weak dispute-resolution mechanisms, and hardly constrains the use of the federal spending power.[15]

In part, the outcome can be explained by the initial position of the provinces, which did not include an opting-out formula. Contrary to Quebec, many provinces wanted less to develop their own social programs than to be heard in the planning of pan-Canadian policies.[16] Many also distrusted their ally, the Quebec government, more than their counterpart, the federal government. These divergences do not explain, however, the distance between the pre-Saskatoon interprovincial position and the final agreement. A popular, and quite plausible, interpretation is that the provinces accepted the agreement in exchange for enhanced health financing and for a new equalization formula, long demanded by the largest and wealthiest provinces. There is no doubt that financial considerations played a role. Still, given the public pressure for better health funding and the difficulty, for the federal government, of supporting health services without going through the provinces, improved financing was likely in any case. A new equalization formula was also to be expected, if not right away, at least in the years to come. The different factors, however, added up, as they did many times before.[17] Governments from the small provinces wanted a strong central government; all except Quebec accepted, indeed demanded, a pan-Canadian vision; Quebec was not trusted as an ally; and provincial politicians knew citizens favoured Ottawa on these questions.

Whatever the case, it can still be concluded that there was a collaborative outcome in the case of the SUFA since it was negotiated and agreed upon by the different parties, except Quebec. Consider, however, how closely the process fits with Keohane's understanding of hegemonic cooperation, "which relies on a dominant power making rules and providing incentives for others to conform with those rules."[18] Hegemonic cooperation, explains Keohane, "is not a contradiction in terms." It simply integrates the fact that cooperation emerges out of conflicts, and not necessarily of conflicts among equals.[19] The notion fits oddly with the idea of non-hierarchical collaboration, but it corresponds fairly well to the course of events in Canada. A negotiation among equals would centre on the credibility of mutual commitments, as each partner limits its own autonomy to reduce uncertainty about the actions of others.[20] Hegemonic cooperation, on the contrary, is likely to leave the less powerful parties uncertain about a dominant power that basically controls the rules of the game. Because it has failed to enunciate a clear overarching view or a well-defined set of principles, notes Harvey Lazar, "the federal government's behaviour is difficult to predict, making it an uncertain and at times unreliable partner for the provinces."[21] This uncertainty, which in recent months has been manifest in various ill-fated improvisations, can hardly be seen as an indicator of non-hierarchical collaboration.

There is another way, however, in which collaborative federalism can be understood as non-hierarchical. In the language of the new theories of public management, the formal

---

15. Noël, "General Study of the Framework Agreement," 13–17.

16. Alain Noël, "Les trois unions sociales," *Policy Options-Options politiques* 19, no. 9 (November 1998): 26–29.

17. Richard Simeon, *Federal-Provincial Diplomacy: The Making of Recent Policy in Canada* (Toronto: University of Toronto Press, 1972), 89, 164, 175, 181–82, 207–8, 213, and 232–34; Claude Morin, *Le combat québécois* (Montréal: Boréal, 1973), 83–90.

18. Keohane, *After Hegemony*, 183.

19. Ibid., 55.

20. Andrew Moravcsik, *The Choice for Europe: Social Purpose and State Power from Messina to Maastricht* (Ithaca: Cornell University Press, 1998), 9.

21. Lazar, "Non-Constitutional Renewal," 10. See also: Harvey Lazar, "In Search of a New Mission Statement for Canadian Federalism," in Lazar (ed.), *Canada: The State of the Federation 1999/2000*, 5, 27–28.

hierarchy of the Weberian bureaucracy should be, as much as possible, replaced by the non-hierarchical logic of the market. The conventional bureaucratic chain of command guarantees democratic accountability, neutrality and continuity, but it also creates rigidities and perverse incentives. The new public management proposes to focus on outcomes rather than on process, and to let autonomous agents provide public services.[22] This is precisely the logic of collaborative federalism. The various collaborative arrangements proposed by the federal government are non-hierarchical in the sense that they replace the traditional logic of public administration by that of alternative delivery systems. "Under these arrangements," explains the 1999 report of the Auditor General,

> the federal government involves external partners in the planning, design and achievement of federal objectives, replacing delivery by federal employees, contractors or agents. These partners are not accountable to ministers or Parliament.

They can be other governments, but also private firms or voluntary organizations.[23] In this perspective, the absence of hierarchy only refers to the absence of a conventional chain of command. It does not mean all partners are equal or have an equal say. The opposite may, in fact, be true.

Indeed, the new public management clearly distinguishes the role of the central state from that of its agents, be they subunit governments or private actors. The central state, goes the standard slogan, should be "steering not rowing." It should set the objectives and define the desired outcomes and let others do the implementation. Service providers will have some autonomy, but they will be held accountable with regular evaluations from above, based on pre-established performance indicators.[24] Transposed to the Canadian federal context, this logic is odd but revealing. It associates democratically accountable provincial governments to private or voluntary sector service providers that are in a principal-agent relationship with the federal government. Like other agents, provinces row for the federal government, which steers and sees that they row in the right direction, at the appropriate rhythm and with sufficient energy.

To a large extent, the new public management remains an ideology, a rhetorical point of view more than an achievement. The implementation of the proposed reforms is difficult and fraught with contradictions and, at least in Canada, it is not very advanced.[25] In intergovernmental relations, in particular, the federal government has not abandoned completely the idea of rowing as well as steering, and the provinces remain more than ordinary partners. Still, just as it does away with the conventional bureaucratic emphasis on legal constraints and formal procedures, the adoption of a new public management rhetoric tends to dismiss the logic of federalism. The division of powers matters less than concrete results, and policies can best be judged by their outcomes. This is why the sharing of information and the development of performance indicators become so important. The logic is akin to that of subsidiarity, a concept that was embraced for a while, but later dropped, by the federal

---

22. François-Xavier Merrien, "La Nouvelle Gestion publique: un concept mythique," *Lien social et politiques* 41 (printemps 1999): 95–97.

23. Auditor General of Canada, *Report* (Ottawa: Auditor General of Canada, November 1999), 23-5 and 23-8.

24. Merrien, "La Nouvelle Gestion publique," 99.

25. Donald J. Savoie, "Public Administration: A Profession Looking for a Home," in Laurent Dobuzinskis, Michael Howlett, and David Laycock (eds.), *Policy Studies in Canada: The State of the Art* (Toronto: University of Toronto Press, 1996), 135–42; Peter Aucoin, *The New Public Management: Canada in Comparative Perspective* (Montreal: Institute for Research on Public Policy, 1995), 3, 15, 250.

government.[26] It is also in tune with an important majoritarian impulse in English Canada, whereby "what works" and "getting things done" often seem to matter more than respect for the federal principle.[27]

The afederal character of the new public management explains why observers diverge in their evaluation of the centralizing or decentralizing impact of collaborative federalism. Many see the overall pattern as obviously decentralizing, either toward the market or toward the provinces.[28] Others present a more prudent evaluation, arguing various outcomes remain possible.[29] Some, particularly in Quebec, interpret the SUFA and other Canada-wide initiatives as indicative of "an increased preponderance of the federal government in social policy."[30]

There is more to these different evaluations than the various standpoints of the observers. These divergences have to do, as well, with the peculiar impact of the new public management on the distribution of power between different orders of government. Paul Hoggett, who studied the introduction of public administration reforms in the United Kingdom, notes that the new models of operational decentralization were promoted by the same Conservative politicians who had "created one of the most centralized forms of government Britain had experienced this century."[31] Operational decentralization, Hoggett argues, "served to reinforce centralization processes." Implementation has been devolved but "control over policy and the allocation of resources had become increasingly concentrated." "Performance-based funding," in particular, has proven to be a powerful tool of central control. According to Hoggett, the new, presumably decentralizing, organizational approaches were "harnessed to a political project which was designed to destroy virtually all alternative power bases within society which might challenge Conservative hegemony."[32] In countries

26. Gilles Paquet notes that the word "subsidiarity" was introduced in federal discourse in 1996, but had been dropped by 1999. He argues, correctly I believe, that the federal government nevertheless maintains "a subsidiarity agenda that does not dare to say its name." Gilles Paquet, "Tectonic Changes in Canadian Governance," in Leslie A. Pal (ed.), *How Ottawa Spends 1999-2000; Shape Shifting: Canadian Governance toward the Twenty-first Century* (Toronto: Oxford University Press, 1999), 108. For a broader critical discussion of the use of the concept of subsidiarity in Canada, see Alain Noël, "The Federal Principle, Solidarity and Partnership," in Roger Gibbins and Guy Laforest (eds.), *Beyond the Impasse: Toward Reconciliation* (Montreal: Institute for Research on Public Policy, 1998): 241–72.

27. Noël, "General Study of the Framework Agreement," 31–32.

28. Leslie A. Pal, "Shape Shifting: Canadian Governance toward the Twenty-first Century," in Pal (ed.), *How Ottawa Spends 1999–2000*, 10; Thomas J. Courchene, "In Praise of Provincial Ascendency," *Policy Options-Options politiques* 19, no. 9 (November 1998): 30–33; Gérard Boismenu and Jane Jenson, "A Social Union or a Federal State? Competing Visions of Intergovernmental Relations in the New Liberal Era," in Leslie A. Pal (ed.), *How Ottawa Spends 1998–99; Balancing Act: The Post-Deficit Mandate* (Toronto: Oxford University Press, 1998), 60–61; Herman Bakvis, "Federalism, New Public Management, and Labour-Market Development," in Patrick C. Fafard and Douglas M. Brown (eds.), *Canada: The State of the Federation 1996* (Kingston: Institute of Intergovernmental Relations, 1996), 153.

29. Harvey Lazar and Tom McIntosh, "How Canadians Connect: State, Economy, Citizenship and Society," in Harvey Lazar and Tom McIntosh (eds.), *Canada: The State of the Federation 1998/99; How Canadians Connect* (Kingston: Institute of Intergovernmental Relations, 1999), 27–30; Keith G. Banting, "Social Citizenship and the Social Union in Canada," *Policy Options-Options politiques* 19, no. 9 (November 1998): 33–36.

30. Claude Ryan, "The Agreement on the Canadian Social Union as Seen by a Quebec Federalist," in Gagnon and Segal (eds.), *The Canadian Social Union without Quebec*, 221; see also François Rocher and Christian Rouillard, "Using the Concept of Deconcentration to Overcome the Centralization/Decentralization Dichotomy: Thoughts on Recent Constitutional and Political Reform," in Fafard and Brown (eds.), *Canada: The State of the Federation 1996*, 126; and Jean-François Lisée, *Sortie de secours: Comment échapper au déclin du Québec* (Montréal: Boréal, 2000), 91–115.

31. Paul Hoggett, "New Modes of Control in the Public Service," *Public Administration* 74, no. 1 (Spring 1996): 18.

32. Ibid., 18–19.

like Germany and Denmark, where such alternative power bases were better established — whether in the public service or in federal, corporatist, or local arrangements — new public management proposals simply failed.[33] In other words, one needs a strong centralizing government to establish new forms of non-hierarchical collaboration inspired by the new public management, and if these reforms succeed, central control tends to be enhanced.[34] The success of decentralization, understood in this way, bodes well for centralization, understood in a more conventional fashion.

At this point, we could accept as a relevant description of current trends the idea that Canadian federalism is becoming more collaborative, insofar as more collaboration is indeed taking place. This collaboration, however, is hardly non-hierarchical. For one thing, when important interests are at stake, the pattern is more akin to hegemonic cooperation than to a negotiation among equals seeking to reduce uncertainty. In addition, the logic of the new public management that informs collaborative federalism clearly places the federal government at the top, in control of a vessel where provinces, like other agents, are expected to row in the same direction. It takes a strong central government to impose this "non-hierarchical" logic on the various social and political actors.

But if collaborative federalism cannot be understood as non-hierarchical, what is it exactly? A good way to make sense of this new form of intergovernmental relations is to understand it not as a specific form of relationships among governments (disentangled or not, hierarchical or not), but rather as a more or less institutionalized governance structure, largely defined by what J. Stefan Dupré called "intragovernmental considerations." Cabinets, argued Dupré, are the "key engine(s) of the state," and they "can operate in vastly different ways."[35] From the 1920s to the 1960s, the "departmentalized cabinet" left much autonomy to ministers and officials responsible for a given portfolio and it facilitated intergovernmental cooperation along functional lines. This was the era of cooperative federalism. In the mid-1960s, the rise of the "institutionalized cabinet" and of central agencies encouraged the formulation of more encompassing priorities and objectives and made intergovernmental relations more visible and competitive. First Ministers' Conferences became the main instrument and the constitution the main issue.[36] Executive federalism, as it would be called, prevailed definitively by 1980, when Prime Minister Pierre Elliott Trudeau declared the end of cooperative federalism and announced more competitive relationships. Informed by an overarching vision of the federation, Trudeau "tested the limits of federal power in field after field" and effectively transformed the constitution and the country.[37] Later attempts at reconciliation, undertaken by the Conservatives in the 1980s and early 1990s, failed to reform a legacy that took hold solidly in Canada outside Quebec.

Meanwhile, the structure of power continued to evolve within the federal government (and probably in the provinces as well). The "institutionalized" Cabinet, argues Donald

---

33. Christoph Knill, "Explaining Cross-National Variance in Administrative Reform: Autonomous versus Instrumental Bureaucracies," *Journal of Public Policy* 19, no. 2 (May-June 1999): 113–39; Peter Munk Christiansen, "A Prescription Rejected: Market Solutions to Problems of Public Sector Governance," *Governance* 11, no. 3 (July 1998): 273–95.

34. Neil Carter, "Performance Indicators: 'Backseat Driving' or 'Hands Off' Control?," *Policy and Politics* 17, no. 2 (April 1989): 31–38; B. Guy Peters and Jon Pierre, "Citizens versus the New Public Manager: The Problem of Mutual Empowerment," *Administration and Society* 32, no. 1 (March 2000): 23.

35. J. Stefan Dupré, "Reflections on the Workability of Executive Federalism," in Richard Simeon (ed.), *Intergovernmental Relations*, Volume 63 of the Studies Prepared for the Royal Commission on the Economic Union and Development Prospects for Canada (Toronto: University of Toronto Press, 1985), 2–3.

36. Ibid., 4–5; Simeon and Robinson, *State, Society, and the Development of Canadian Federalism*, 284.

37. Simeon and Robinson, *State, Society, and the Development of Canadian Federalism*, 283, 298.

Savoie, "has joined Parliament as an institution being bypassed... in the late 1990s, effective power rests with the prime minister and a small group of carefully selected courtiers."[38] Decisions, large and small, are taken at the top, often without involving Cabinet or the departments concerned. Chrétien's Verdun speech on national unity at the end of the 1995 referendum campaign, cuts in unemployment insurance, the Millennium Scholarship Fund, the Canada Foundation for Innovation, and a host of other measures significant for intergovernmental relations emanated from the centre, without going through the Cabinet process.[39] Even the introduction in 1995 of the Canada Health and Social Transfer (CHST), which involved $25 billion in transfers to the provinces and gave rise to the social union process, was decided without involving Cabinet.[40]

For intergovernmental relations, this concentration of power has at least three consequences. First, the whole process becomes controlled at the top, because line ministers are not trusted to manage intergovernmental, or other, issues.[41] In some cases, this centralization has the advantage of accelerating or simplifying decision making. Often, however, it leads the government to ignore important regional and functional considerations and to lose sight of issues that are not at the top of the political agenda. For instance, the Millennium Scholarship Fund, the offer to support professional hockey teams, and the clarity bill contradicted other governmental objectives or were advanced despite significant opposition in Cabinet.

Second, this concentration of power makes intergovernmental relations more haphazard and unpredictable. In the absence of a clear, overall vision or strategy, the central government tends to react to circumstances, events or provincial initiatives, forcing the provinces to scramble with the results. The centre, argues Savoie, governs by "bolts of electricity" and "micromanages" the files selected as important by the prime minister.[42] As a result, the provinces have come to see Ottawa as a "most unreliable partner."[43] This impression certainly was not dispelled when Jean Chrétien quipped, in the days preceding the social union agreement, that "sometimes on Monday I feel like giving the provinces more money, and then on Tuesday not."[44] Few statements better capture the implications of court government for intergovernmental relations.

Third, the concentration of power around the prime minister creates a situation where those in charge tend to have "little patience for due process."[45] Unable to develop support for constitutional change in the provinces, Ottawa moved alone, with little success, to recognize Quebec as distinct and to introduce regional constitutional vetoes.[46] Unable to compromise on the social union, the federal government pushed forward a Framework Agreement that will apply to Quebec even though it is not a signatory. Even the process that was created on February 4, 1999, seems disposable. Less than two weeks after the agreement, the federal budget introduced major changes in the CHST that had not been preceded by the formal

---

38. Donald J. Savoie, "The Rise of Court Government in Canada," *Canadian Journal of Political Science* 22, no. 4 (December 1999): 635.

39. Ibid., 639, 647, 657, 663.

40. Donald J. Savoie, *Governing from the Centre: The Concentration of Power in Canadian Politics* (Toronto: University of Toronto Press, 1999), 189.

41. Ibid., 346; Savoie, "The Rise of Court Government in Canada," 639–40.

42. Savoie, *Governing from the Centre*, 153, 358–59.

43. Courchene, "In Praise of Provincial Ascendency," 31.

44. Jean Chrétien, quoted in Paquet, "Tectonic Changes in Canadian Governance," 102.

45. Savoie, "The Rise of Court Government in Canada," 662.

46. Robert A. Young, *The Struggle for Quebec: From Referendum to Referendum?* (Montreal and Kingston: McGill-Queen's University Press, 1999), 95–96.

consultations specified in the SUFA. The fact that the issue had been publicly debated, in a general way, was deemed sufficient to meet the requirements of the SUFA.[47] The $1 billion management failure at Human Resources Development that was unveiled early in 2000 is probably the most spectacular example of this general tendency to disregard due process. "Administrative problems of this nature always exist," simply said the prime minister.[48]

Collaborative federalism is hierarchical. In fact, Canadian federalism has never been more centralized. Power is concentrated not only in Ottawa, but also at the top, in the prime minister's "court." Collaboration occurs, but it is the collaboration of rowing agents who follow the indications of a steering principal whose behaviour is difficult to understand, let alone predict. Negotiations do take place, but they do not involve more or less equal partners seeking to reduce uncertainty. They are defined, instead, by the most powerful player, able to induce others to abide by rules that it can change at will. Collaboration, of course, also takes place without Quebec, the only government that would challenge federal hegemony in a fundamental way.

De Facto Asymmetry?

La différence est un caillou dans l'engrenage de la nation.
   Gérard Bouchard, 1999[49]

Quebec has never been so marginalized in the Canadian federation. In the past, the government of Quebec often maintained a distance in intergovernmental negotiations, but it always remained a critical player. Even in 1981–82, it was only with hesitation and a certain malaise that the provinces, specialists, and Canadian public opinion approved a federal constitutional approach that bypassed the government of Quebec. With the SUFA, a deal without Quebec was reached in just a few days, with little afterthought. More generally, collaborative arrangements progress unabated, with only a footnote to indicate the absence of a central province. In December 1999, a federal Clarity Bill was introduced to empower the federal government to disallow the positive results of a Quebec referendum that would put forward any question mentioning "economic or political arrangements with Canada" or that would produce a majority that Ottawa would deem unclear, in light of any "matters or circumstances it considers to be relevant."[50] This bill, which challenges the powers of Quebec's National Assembly and presents the Quebec electorate as unsophisticated, was broadly supported across Canada, including by the main opposition parties. If this last year is indicative, collaborative federalism does not seem to bode well for Quebeckers.

In English Canada, some observers nevertheless see a silver lining in this evolution. Roger Gibbins, for one, appears particularly optimistic. The SUFA, he writes, "clearly sets Quebec apart from the other provinces." While the other provinces will engage in collaboration with the federal government and abide by its conditions, Quebec "will stand apart, its jurisdictional integrity uncompromised." The Quebec government may still harmonize its programs with those of other provinces, "but it is under no obligation to do so" and can remain

---

47. Noël, "The Social Union Framework Agreement."

48. Jean Chrétien, quoted in Daniel Leblanc, "Multibillion-Dollar Mess Routine, Chrétien Says; Administrative Woes Always Exist, he Argues in Minister's Defence," *Globe and Mail*, February 1, 2000.

49. Gérard Bouchard et Michel Lacombe, *Dialogue sur les pays neufs* (Montréal: Boréal, 1999), 35.

50. Minister of Intergovernmental Affairs, *Bill C-20, An Act to give effect to the requirement for clarity as set out in the opinion of the Supreme Court of Canada in the Quebec Secession Reference*, 3–4 (first reading, The House of Commons of Canada, Second Session, Thirty-Sixth Parliament, December 10, 1999).

autonomous "with no financial risks." Quebec's "political clout in Ottawa and the remaining threat of separatism" gives the province "most favoured nation status in its bilateral, one might say binational, negotiations with the federal government."[51] The result, concludes Gibbins, is remarkable:

> the prime minister has achieved for Quebec what the majority of Quebec nationalists have sought for the past 30 years — a distinct position within the Canadian federal system in which Quebec is not a province like the others but rather has the *de facto* status of a separate national community, dealing one-on-one with the government of Canada.
>
> … Quebec maintains its autonomy, is able to block constitutional change, and is able to use its political leverage in Ottawa to ensure that no financial costs are imposed. … The prime minister may have delivered on the ultimate paradox: an independent Quebec within a strong Canada.[52]

The lack of enthusiasm manifested by Quebeckers raises some doubts about Gibbins' analysis. In Quebec, the most positive assessments of the February 4, 1999, agreement concluded that it basically "changed nothing."[53] At the same time, the SUFA undeniably introduces some *de facto* asymmetry. Could it point in the right direction? Could it lead, incrementally, to a situation more representative of the dual character of the Canadian federation? Probably not.

First, in a federation, as in any institutional arrangements, the formal and informal rules of the game matter, and the capacity to change these rules matters even more. All sides agree that the SUFA is an important change in the rules of the game, since it circumscribes the use of the federal spending power in a novel way. The same is true for the National Child Benefit, which concerns the provinces as well as the federal government, and for the Clarity Bill, which introduces new rules for a future Quebec referendum. In all these cases, the federal and the provincial governments did not seek genuinely the approval of the Quebec government, or even of the official opposition in the National Assembly. This approval hardly seemed to matter. Regardless of the consequences, this capacity to alter the rules unilaterally poses a problem.

A free and respectful multinational society, argues James Tully, allows changes in the rules of mutual recognition, but does not permit unilateral changes in these rules. In Canada, Quebec is not free because constitutional amendments can be adopted without its consent, because it cannot in practice seek constitutional recognition, and because it would be bound, following a referendum, by constitutional rules it has not approved.[54] This is not simply a symbolic or abstract constitutional question. As Tully notes, debates about recognition also define power relations in a society.[55] On a series of questions, Canada now marches on as if Quebec did not exist or did not matter. The SUFA is a case in point. As with the constitution, Quebec will be bound by an agreement it did not demand and did not approve. No matter how the Quebec government uses the situation to act autonomously, the outcome has more to do with domination than with freedom. In the process, the little trust that had been

---

51. Roger Gibbins, "Taking Stock: Canadian Federalism and Its Constitutional Framework," in Pal (ed.), *How Ottawa Spends 1999–2000*, 216–17.

52. Ibid., 217–18.

53. Alain Dubuc, "Signer ou ne pas signer?," *La Presse*, February 5, 1999, B2.

54. James Tully, "Liberté et dévoilement dans les sociétés multinationales," *Globe, Revue internationale d'études québécoises* 2, no. 2 (1999): 15–16, 31.

55. Ibid., 18.

built between the provinces was also seriously undermined.[56] Nothing prevents future changes that would be inimical to Quebec.

Second, Gibbins' argument on *de facto* asymmetry underestimates the importance of the SUFA in legitimizing the federal spending power. Even though the SUFA is only an administrative, time-limited document, it provides the first explicit recognition, by the provinces, of the legitimacy of federal expenditures and standards in areas under their jurisdiction. The fact that this recognition has no legal status is secondary because the issues surrounding the spending power are not primarily legal or constitutional. In most cases, the federal government simply cannot use its spending power without the collaboration of the provinces, since they play a critical role in the definition and implementation of social policy.[57] This is true even for direct transfers to individuals, as can be seen with the Millennium Scholarship Fund or the National Child Benefit, which cannot be implemented without provincial collaboration. In such cases, relative power and negotiations matter more than legal constraints. In a discussion of the Meech Lake Accord, Keith Banting made similar observations and concluded that a consensus on the use of the spending power would strengthen this federal prerogative "far more than a favourable ruling of the Supreme Court ever could."[58] The SUFA fell short of a consensus, but it came as close as ever to the conditions enunciated by Banting. The balance of power has shifted in favour of the federal government, and this certainly does not make Quebec more autonomous in social policy. Indeed, the National Child Benefit indicates how Quebec, even more than the provinces that participate in the discussions, can become a policy taker in areas within its own jurisdictions.

Third, Gibbins underestimates the contribution of the SUFA to a process that is reshaping social policy in Canada. More will be said on this question in the next section, but one example is worth mentioning. With respect to mobility within Canada, the SUFA goes much beyond the previous interprovincial position and calls for the elimination of "any residency-based policies or practices which constrain access to post-secondary education, training, health and social services and social assistance unless they can be demonstrated to be reasonable and consistent with the principles of the Social Union Framework."[59] A new norm, more associated with social policy, is created that goes beyond the logic of free trade and imposes new obligations and constraints on the provinces. Quebec is not a signatory, but this new framework is likely to affect it nevertheless, because it will impose the renegotiation of agreements such as the agreement on Internal Trade, which Quebec has signed.[60] In other words, a new pan-Canadian social framework is emerging and it is unlikely that Quebec can remain unaffected by its norms and constraints.

While it is true that collaborative federalism with a footnote creates a form of *de facto* asymmetry, it is not a form of asymmetry that responds to Quebec's demands for recognition and autonomy. On the contrary, this new brand of federalism changes the rules of the game

---

56. Claude Ryan, in "Four Views of the Social Union," *Policy Options-Options politiques* 20, no. 3 (April 1999): 75; Lazar and McIntosh, "How Canadians Connect," 29.

57. Peter Hogg, "Analysis of the New Spending Power Provision (Section 106A)," in Katherine E. Swinton and Carol J. Rogerson (eds.), *Competing Constitutional Visions: The Meech Lake Accord* (Toronto: Carswell, 1988), 157–58.

58. Keith G. Banting, "Federalism, Social Reform and the Spending Power," *Canadian Public Policy* 14, Supplement (September 1988): S84–S85.

59. Government of Canada and Governments of the Provinces and Territories, *A Framework to Improve the Social Union for Canadians* (Ottawa: n.p., February 4, 1999), 2.

60. Jacques Frémont, "Mobility within Canada," in Gagnon and Segal (eds.), *The Canadian Social Union without Quebec*, 71–91; Lazar, "The Social Union Framework Agreement and the Future of Fiscal Federalism," 105–6; Courchene, *A State of Minds*, 93–95.

without the consent of the Quebec government, it reinforces the federal spending power, and it contributes to advance a new pan-Canadian vision of social policy that will affect Quebec, with or without its approval. The only autonomy that is enhanced for Quebec is the autonomy of the footnote, the negative autonomy of the nonparticipant. The Quebec government can be an irritant in the workings of Canadian federalism, a grain of sand in the mechanics of Canadian nationalism, but this is hardly an achievement worth celebrating.

The problem with collaborative federalism with a footnote is less a lack of asymmetry than a lack of federalism. Canada was created as a federation precisely because federalism allowed different peoples to live together and, at the same time, separately. More than provinces, the peoples involved were, initially, the peoples of Lower and Upper Canada, the French and the English Canadians. The need to accommodate the two remains the most critical dimension of federalism in Canada. When they opted for the politics of the footnote, the governments of this country chose an easy way out, but left unattended this central imperative, which made federalism necessary in Canada.

Asymmetry or reconciliation will not be obtained as unplanned bonuses for signing an agreement without Quebec. In the 1960s, Quebec obtained a *de facto* special status in social policy, but lost it a few years later when the federal government decided to erase anything that suggested that there were two distinct nations in Canada.[61] Existential questions such as this one are unlikely to be settled "by stealth," to use an expression familiar to social policy analysts. The issue that makes asymmetry necessary is not social policy autonomy per se, but rather recognition, and recognition cannot be granted unknowingly, by accident.

A Third Way?

I believe we know what is required to address the main problems that we face at this moment.
    Allan Rock, Minister of Health, January 27, 2000[62]

The SUFA and collaborative federalism are often presented as alternatives to the old, presumably dated, debates about the division of powers or about centralization and decentralization.[63] From now on, the test of success would be less whether intergovernmental arrangements seem to work for governments, and more whether they produce satisfactory results for citizens. This reasoning, often associated with the notion of subsidiarity, is a very common form of wishful thinking. Policies, however, are never detached from processes. Collaborative federalism with a footnote does not simply "work for Canadians." It makes some policy choices easier than others. It may well contribute, in particular, to develop Canadian social policies around persons and through income taxes rather than around places and through services. Whether or not this is the best, or only, possible outcome appears highly debatable.

In recent years, federal social policies and social policy instruments have changed significantly. In 1995, the creation of the CHST pooled together, with little conditions except for health services, the transfers to the provinces devoted to health, social assistance and social

---

61. Simeon, *Federal-Provincial Diplomacy*, 171–72; Yves Vaillancourt, "Le régime d'assistance publique du Canada: perspective québécoise" (Thèse présentée à la Faculté des études supérieures en vue de l'obtention du grade de Ph.D. en science politique, Université de Montréal, 1992), 340–44; Kenneth McRoberts, *Misconceiving Canada: The Struggle for National Unity* (Toronto: Oxford University Press, 1997), 141–42.

62. Allan Rock, quoted in Anne McIlroy, "Rock Plans Urgent Drive to Overhaul Health Care: Patient Waiting Lists, National Home Care Top His Agenda," *Globe and Mail*, January 27, 2000, A1.

63. See, for instance, Reg Whitaker, "The Changing Canadian State," in Lazar and McIntosh (eds.), *Canada: The State of the Federation 1998/99*, 39; Paquet, "Tectonic Changes in Canadian Governance," 75–111.

services, and post-secondary education. In February 1999, a new, per capita rule was designed for these pooled social transfers. Concretely, this new rule implied that the federal government had simply left the social assistance field, the least popular and least rewarding politically of its previous transfers. Nominally, some transfers are still associated with social assistance, but CHST transfers are now pooled and blind to social conditions and they can be used for practically any aim. Per capita, Alberta will now get almost as much social assistance money as, say, Quebec or Newfoundland. One could argue that equalization payments correct this, but equalization is not a social policy, it is simply a means to provide the different provincial governments with comparable resources. In a context where employment insurance covers less and less unemployed persons, the federal government actually withdraws transfers that used to be devoted to social assistance in high unemployment provinces. Once it is basically on a per capita basis and blind to social conditions, it is hard to see a social rationale for the CHST.[64]

This movement away from social assistance transfers, along with the creation of the National Child Benefit, of the Millenium Scholarship Fund and of a host of boutique programs, can be associated with an evolution that John Kincaid, an American federalism scholar, has called the movement from places to persons.[65] The Canadian government, like its American counterpart, has become less interested in transfers to the provinces and more attracted by direct or fiscal transfers to groups or individuals. This evolution is not entirely new, and it certainly does not tell the whole story. Transfers to the provinces remain very important and largely unconditional.[66] In health and post-secondary education, in particular, such a transition remains limited because the federal government cannot run hospitals or universities. Still, the trend can be observed in Allan Rock's various efforts to reaffirm federal leadership and visibility in health policy, as well as in the creation of various boutique programs supporting research, innovation or higher education. In all these cases, the federal government attempts to circumvent the provinces to reach persons and institutions directly.

In social assistance, the move is decisive. Provinces will receive smaller transfers, unrelated to their social situation, but individuals will receive cheques with a large maple leaf on the front. The federal money will be for their children. If their general financial situation deteriorates, however, it will remain their province's responsibility. The provinces will also have to think twice before providing job training to these persons. If they have not qualified for employment insurance in recent years — an increasingly likely scenario — no federal money will go toward their training. The federal government, after all, must be accountable for the funds it collects through employment insurance contributions. Other than miscellaneous federal projects, they should not be used for purposes unrelated to unemployment. Canadians will feel reassured knowing that Human Resources Development keeps a watchful eye on free-spending provinces, which may be tempted to divest employment insurance money to train "undeserving" social assistance recipients.

It is too early to evaluate the full consequences of this move from places to persons. Because the federal government can more easily send cheques than provide social services and is more adept at promoting negative (removing barriers) than positive (creating institutions) integration, the impact will be redistributive but not necessarily innovative.[67]

---

64. Serge Coulombe and Marcel Mérette, "Fiscal Needs and the CHST Per Capita Division Rule," *Canadian Tax Journal* 48, no. 2 (2000): 340–55.

65. John Kincaid, "De Facto Devolution and Urban Defunding: The Priority of Persons over Places," *Journal of Urban Affairs* 21, no. 2 (1999).

66. Lazar, "In Search of a New Mission Statement for Canadian Fiscal Federalism," 21, 27.

67. Thomas J. Courchene, *Celebrating Flexibility: An Interpretive Essay on the Evolution of Canadian Federalism* (Toronto: C.D. Howe Institute, 1995), 61.

Various persons will see their situation improved or worsened, but better practices or institutions will not necessarily follow. Fiscal deductions for child care, for instance, may support community-based or private services; as they exist now, they discourage the universal model adopted in Quebec.

Canada will have a more integrated market governed by a more present central state, but it may have difficulties in fostering various models of community-based, integrated and enabling services.[68] Indeed, the concentration of power identified above implies the prime minister and the minister of finance now stand as the almost unchallenged social policy leaders. Court government will tend to circumvent the provinces, the main social actors and a good part of the policy community.[69] Finance will promote income and tax-based policies aimed at individuals, and particularly at individual children, at the expense of community-based and service-oriented options. Other voices will be heard in and around Ottawa, regarding health care in particular, but they are unlikely to be as powerful in setting the agenda.

In a more general way, collaborative federalism with a footnote corresponds to a certain idea of the politics of the "Third Way." Important ideas are currently developed by social-democrats under the Third Way umbrella. There is a tendency, however, to replace Margaret Thatcher's TINA ("There is no alternative") by a Third Way TIBOO ("There is but only one"). The new discourse on social investment, which is put forward at the Organization for Economic Cooperation and Development (OECD) and in most capitals, tends to present choices as mostly technical and best defined by central governments. In the social-democratic tradition, however, there is a powerful current that emphasizes local autonomy, genuine empowerment, and the superiority of reforms defined from below.[70] In English Canada, this current has been trumped by nationalism and the Left has promoted centralization and national standards more than autonomy and empowerment.[71] This explains why collaborative federalism with a footnote is perceived positively on the left in Canada, even though it does not point in an obvious way in the direction of progressive reforms. One hope is that Quebec, which is more progressive than other provinces on most social questions, will forge ahead and create something like a distinct model, which could be emulated. This is the case, in my opinion, with family policy. But, again, the social union does not make such an evolution easy.

Conclusion

Deviens-tu c'que t'as voulu?/Deviens-tu c'que t'avais vu?/
Deviens-tu c'que t'aurais pu?/T'as-tu fait c'qu'y aurait fallu?
    Daniel Boucher, *Deviens-tu c'que t'as voulu?*, 1999

The SUFA of February 4, 1999, was particularly regrettable because it was a missed opportunity, a lost occasion to take advantage of important concessions that had been accepted by the different provinces. Why was this occasion missed? Why was it so important to sign a deal rapidly, without taking the time to build on these compromises? Apparently, a deal had to be signed because Jean Chrétien and his court had had enough. They wanted an agreement

---

68. Alain Noël, "Is Decentralization Conservative? Federalism and the Contemporary Debate on the Canadian Welfare State," in Robert Young (ed.), *Stretching the Federation: The Art of the State in Canada* (Kingston: Institute of Intergovernmental Relations, 1999), 212–17.

69. Jane Jenson, with Sherry Thompson, *Comparative Family Policy: Six Provincial Stories*, CPRN Study No. F-08 (Ottawa: Canadian Policy Research Networks, 1999), 38.

70. Alain Noël, "Vers un nouvel État-providence? Enjeux démocratiques," *Politique et sociétés* 30 (automne 1996): 3–27.

71. Noël, "Is Decentralization Conservative?," 210–14.

right away, and had the wherewithal to draft it and pay for it. As a result, what can be called, for lack of a better expression, collaborative federalism with a footnote, was entrenched, institutionalized.

This intergovernmental arrangement is hierarchical in at least three ways. First, it was defined in Ottawa and pushed forward in a negotiation that had more to do with hegemonic cooperation than with multilateralism. Second, it is inspired by the falsely non-hierarchical logic of the new public management, where the centre steers and the provinces row. Third, it constitutes an intergovernmental regime that corresponds well to the logic of court government, a system of government that concentrates power at the top, that emphasizes short-term solutions, and that pays little attention to formal rules and due process.

Despite the footnote, collaborative federalism does not deliver meaningful asymmetry. The SUFA demonstrated, once again, how the rules of the game can be changed without the consent of Quebec. It also reinforced the legitimacy of one of Ottawa's main tools in social policy, the spending power. Finally, it further defined and institutionalized a pan-Canadian vision of social policy that leaves little room for autonomy or difference. This intergovernmental regime is, to some extent, asymmetric, but it does not constitute asymmetric federalism, because it does not respect the federal principle, as it was defined in Canadian history.

For social policy, only time will tell what the outcome will be, but the Department of Finance is more likely than provinces or communities to have a say in delineating this outcome. On these questions, Finance is likely to ignore what Swedish political scientist Bo Rothstein has called "the central message of Italian double entry bookkeeping," namely that, in social policy, redistribution is defined not only by what individuals receive but also by what they contribute.[72] In other words, the contemporary calculus of individual benefits, very present in federal discussions of family policy, tends to lose sight of the broader picture. Universal programs or services are helpful not only because they create equal citizenship rights, but also because they make citizens more willing to pay a fair share of taxes.

As a way to conclude, it is worth bringing back the new public management image of steering and rowing. As explained above, this image provides a fair representation of collaborative federalism. It constitutes, however, a very poor and uninspiring representation for a country like Canada, especially if we add that one partner does not sing the same rowing song and that the hand at the helm appears strong but capricious. A not so different, but much more interesting image is offered by Bill Reid's sculpture, *The Spirit of Haida Gwaii*, as evoked by James Tully. Reid explains his sculpture of a black canoe carrying very diverse partners in these words:

> Here we are at last, a long way from Haida Gwaii, not too sure where we are or where we're going, still squabbling and vying for position in the boat, but somehow managing to appear to be heading in some direction. At least the paddles are together, and the man in the middle seems to have some vision of what's to come.[73]

In my opinion, this sophisticated and open perspective is much more relevant to Canadian federalism than the steering and rowing image of the new public management. It cannot be found, however, in the SUFA.

Is such a vision now out of reach for Canada? During the discussion, at a December 1999 Institute for Research on Public Policy (IRPP) roundtable on Canadian federalism, Claude

---

72. Bo Rothstein, *Just Institutions Matter: The Moral and Political Logic of the Universal Welfare State* (Cambridge: Cambridge University Press, 1998), 148.

73. Bill Reid, quoted in James Tully, *Strange Multiplicity: Constitutionalism in an Age of Diversity* (Cambridge: Cambridge University Press, 1995), 23.

Ryan observed that in the last few decades he had attended many of these well-intended meetings on federalism. It takes a lot of patience, he said, to keep reiterating, year after year and without success, the same basic arguments. This was a sad comment, from a respected Quebec federalist who has devoted all of his professional life to public affairs. Being less committed to the Canadian idea, and less patient, I think, than Claude Ryan, I wondered at the time where I would be and what I would say at his age. I am not sure I want to answer this question.

CHAPTER THREE

Getting Engaged:
Strengthening the SUFA through Citizen Engagement[1]

Matthew Mendelsohn and John McLean

Introduction

The Social Union Framework Agreement (SUFA) makes a commitment to engage Canadians on social policy, but how this commitment can be implemented is open to question. The two animating themes of the SUFA appear to be intergovernmental cooperation and public participation, yet these principles tend to be in direct conflict. Despite the apparent conflict between these two principles, both reflect Canadian values and we suggest that both can be accommodated in institutional design.

We argue that citizen engagement must be a formal and organized part of the SUFA. Past consultation exercises by governments on many issues have suffered from their ad hoc nature, which has undermined their impact because often citizens did not know of their existence, could not easily track their impact on decision making, and were unconvinced of their sincerity. Only through integrating citizen engagement exercises formally, accompanied by government commitments to treat processes seriously, can engagement exercises fulfil their purposes. Through such public processes, the SUFA could be reinforced and could become an important component of Canadian identity.

This chapter first examines the strong commitment to citizen engagement in the SUFA, and then describes how the principle of popular participation is often seen to be in conflict with intergovernmental collaboration. We then discuss the principles of citizen engagement, with particular reference to their application to intergovernmental policies, and then explain why engagement is necessary, again with particular reference to the area of intergovernmental social policies. In the next section we discuss how engagement processes can actually be implemented, taking into consideration citizens' four distinct roles: consumers of government services, clients of government programs, bearers of rights, and democratic actors (the latter including the roles of "decision maker" and "informed voter"). We conclude by offering our recommendations in regards to citizen engagement and the SUFA.

---

1. We would like to thank Tom McIntosh and Patrick Fafard for inviting us to the Saskatchewan Institute of Public Policy's Forum on the Social Union and making the chapter possible. We sincerely thank Leslie Seidle and Allan Tupper for their detailed comments on an earlier draft of this chapter. We would also like to thank Keith Banting, Harvey Lazar, and Debbie Cook whose thoughts have strengthened our own argumentation.

Assessing the Commitments to Citizen Engagement

There are five strong commitments in the SUFA to citizen engagement:

> • promote the full and active participation of all Canadians in Canada's social and economic life;

> • work in partnership with individuals, families, communities, voluntary organisations, business and labour, and ensure appropriate opportunities for Canadians to have meaningful input into social policies and programs;

> • ensure effective mechanisms for Canadians to participate in developing social priorities and reviewing outcomes;

> • have in place appropriate mechanisms for citizens to appeal unfair administrative practices and bring complaints about access and service;

> • this review [of the SUFA within three years] will ensure significant opportunities for feedback from Canadians.

The first two of these commitments — referred to in this chapter as the "*promoting full participation*" and "*meaningful input into policies*" provisions — appear in the introductory "Principles" section. The third and fourth commitments — referred to in this chapter as the "*effective mechanisms for participation*" and "*mechanisms for appeal*" provisions — appear later in the "Informing Canadians — Public Accountability and Transparency" section. The fifth — referred to as the "*opportunities for feedback*" provision — is found in the final section of the SUFA dealing with its review.

In addition to these five principles, there is also an entire section of the SUFA devoted to commitments on accountability and transparency. This section, and others, include commitments to: monitor and measure outcomes of social programs and report regularly to constituents on performance; publicly recognize and explain the respective roles and contributions of governments; report publicly on citizens' appeals and complaints; and report publicly on the nature of intergovernmental disputes and their resolution (referred to collectively in this chapter as the "*accountability*" provisions). If applied, these accountability provisions are important in that they provide visibility to the SUFA and provide citizens and interest groups with better quality information concerning the commitments and actions of governments.

Although these provisions are somewhat broad, they are quite strong in their commitment to citizen engagement, with the "meaningful input into policies" and "effective mechanisms for participation" particularly explicit. There is no doubt that some of these provisions are formulated in quite general terms and will be difficult to operationalize,[2] yet this is no different from many of the other provisions in the SUFA, drafted to be general statements of intent with the actual details to be worked out later. The lack of detail contained within the commitments in the SUFA is due in part to the fact that they are intended to apply to all areas of social policy, each of which may require unique processes for engagement. Moreover, the commitments may lack precision because many governments are new to the area of citizen engagement and may be relatively unfamiliar with the various models of engagement or how precisely they could be advantageously deployed in the area of social policy development.

---

2. In a preliminary survey administered to social policy experts, conducted by John McLean and Harvey Lazar, most of these provisions were seen to be quite ambiguous and quite difficult to achieve. Some of the provisions, however, in particular the "mechanisms for appeal" and the "opportunities for feedback," were judged to be quite precise and reasonably easy to achieve. Likewise, many of the "accountability" provisions were seen to be precise, although in most cases a majority of respondents found that they would be difficult to achieve. See John McLean and Harvey Lazar, *Assessing the Provisions of the Social Union Framework Agreement*, Institute of Intergovernmental Relations, Working Paper Series (Kingston: Institute of Intergovernmental Relations, forthcoming).

In short, the open-ended nature of the commitments to citizen engagement is consistent with the character of other provisions within the SUFA and should not be taken as an indication that governments were insincere in their commitment to public involvement. It now falls to the larger policy community and the public service to define detailed models of engagement which permit the realization of the broad engagement goals set out in the SUFA.

One must first acknowledge that including public involvement in intergovernmental files is particularly challenging. The presence of citizen engagement can threaten the ability of governments to manage conflicts and these public engagement processes can undermine governments' abilities to adopt the strategic negotiating positions that they often believe to be essential for the protection of their interests. Because there is often a great deal of difficulty reaching intergovernmental agreements, there is a reluctance to include a greater number of actors who could potentially block agreement. Governments hesitate to include the public at the beginning of the process because they want to maintain control and freedom of manoeuvrability in their negotiating positions, and hesitate to do so at the end of the policy process because citizens might question the agreement and undermine the delicate balances that have been so painstakingly negotiated. These quite real challenges to the viability of citizen engagement on intergovernmental policy must be successfully dealt with before one can seriously consider including the public.

Combining Citizen Engagement and Intergovernmental Collaboration in the SUFA

Models of federalism generally, and in Canada specifically, have tended to contrast democracy and citizen participation on the one hand with intergovernmentalism and guardianship on the other. Many have tended to assume, with good reason, that intergovernmentalism leads to elite-level decision making and makes public participation difficult.[3] The conflict between participatory and federal structures has long been noted in Canada, and Canadian decision making has been dominated far more by an interest in intergovernmental elite bargaining than with public input or popular sovereignty.[4] Decision making by the executive is inherently less open to public debate than legislation made through the legislative process, and democratic accountability suffers when authority is transferred away from legislatures to executive bargaining.[5] Intergovernmental negotiations are one of the few areas of policy, along with monetary policy and international relations, that are highly resistant to citizen engagement and more democratic public administration.

Yet the SUFA contains commitments to both public participation and intergovernmental cooperation. Although both elements can be seen as the SUFA's animating principles, there is no acknowledgement in the document of the tension between them, nor any acknowledgement that they represent quite different models of democratic governance, one of which is almost entirely alien to Canadian practice. The SUFA likewise contains no suggestion for resolving the contradictions between the two.

The balancing act between these two principles makes sense if one takes into consideration public attitudes and political culture. In the past thirty years there has been an increase in citizens' confidence in their own democratic abilities and a decline in their confidence in

3. Donald Smiley, "An Outsider's Observations of Federal-Provincial Relations among Consenting Adults," in Richard Simeon (ed.), *Confrontation and Collaboration: Intergovernmental Relations in Canada Today* (Toronto: Institute of Public Administration of Canada, 1979).

4. Reginald Whitaker, *Federalism and Democratic Theory*, Institute of Intergovernmental Relations Discussion Paper No. 17 (Kingston: Institute of Intergovernmental Relations, 1983).

5. Albert Breton, "Supplementary Statement," *Royal Commission on the Economic Union and Development Prospects for Canada*, volume 3 (Ottawa: n.p., 1985).

government, producing what has variously been labeled a decline of deference or a democratic deficit.[6] This has produced various calls for more public participation in decision making and the commitments to citizen engagement in the SUFA respond to these trends. Yet at the same time, public opinion has little patience for traditional conflictual models of intergovernmental bargaining. This strong inclination in public attitudes in favor of more cooperative arrangements has shown up consistently in polls for several years,[7] and the SUFA's nod toward increased collaborative federalism responds to this.

If the SUFA becomes more formally implemented — and this remains very much in doubt — one of two things will occur. Intergovernmental cooperation will come to structure decision making at the expense of citizen engagement, an outcome that would certainly be consistent with the history of intergovernmental relations in Canada. Alternatively, it is possible that governments will resist — or be forced to resist — this temptation and instead will develop models of public participation suitable for collaborative intergovernmental decision making.

We do not underestimate the challenge of combining these two elements. A preliminary survey of other federations, including the European Union, Australia, the United States, Switzerland, and Germany, reveals that although there are many examples of public consultation, there are very few examples of consultation in policy areas that are subject to intergovernmental negotiation.[8] Of these isolated examples, none are on the same scale as those envisioned in the SUFA commitments, which apply to a wide range of social policy issues and are not limited to "one-time" exercises in particular policy fields. Canada's SUFA commitments to citizen engagement appear to be quite unique and broader than commitments found elsewhere, suggesting that the operationalization of the commitments will not be a simple matter of applying models from elsewhere.

The Principles of Citizen Engagement for Intergovernmental Relations

Citizen engagement is different than traditional consultation because ordinary citizens, along with traditional decision makers (public servants, interest groups, and elected representatives) have a say in outcomes. While traditional consultations tend to provide a snapshot of public opinion at a particular moment in time, engagement is deliberative, interactive, and ongoing, much like government decision making. Citizen engagement mechanisms permit citizens not only to be in the opening stage of decision making (information sharing, surveying the environment) and the closing stage (accountability, reporting, assessing outcomes) but also in the middle stage where choices are actually made. Citizen engagement should be understood as an ongoing component of decision making which includes two-way communications and is distinguished from the two previous models of consultation: (1) public meetings at which officials listen to the public's views and concerns, but then retire to make decisions amongst themselves ("venting" processes); or (2) public meetings during which officials provide information and/or justification for decisions ("telling and selling" processes).

In contrast to these traditional public consultations, engagement processes encompass dialogue and issue recommendations based on a real array of trade-offs and choices. Ideally, they are not restricted to a single event, they provide neutral spaces for deliberation, government

---

6. Neil Nevitte, *The Decline of Deference* (Toronto: Broadview, 1996).

7. Pollara/CROP Surveys, October 1996, Privy Council Office. Results available from Matthew Mendelsohn.

8. See Matthew Mendelsohn and John McLean, "Reconcilable Differences: Public Participation and Intergovernmentalism in Canada," in David Stewart and Paul Thomas (eds.), *Federalism and Democracy* (Winnipeg: University of Manitoba Press, forthcoming).

options must be open to change, and the process must be publicly accountable, which includes assured listening by decision makers. What distinguishes citizen engagement is the interactive, co-decisional nature of the process. Although one can never attain an "ideal speech situation," one can build institutions and processes governed less by strategic manipulation and coercion.[9] Citizen engagement can therefore be thought of as openended yet structured public dialogue contributing to specific decisions in a transparent and publicly accountable manner.[10]

Citizen engagement exercises feature a prominent role for elites — including public servants and experts — in an attempt to mirror traditional decision-making processes. Those interested in democratizing intergovernmental relations through citizen engagement also recognize that processes would feature an increased role for elected representatives, in addition to the general public.

There are a number of principles that contribute to successful citizen engagement processes. These include: (1) a genuine commitment from governments to the process, which could include reporting on how the views emerging from citizen engagement processes were taken into account in final decisions; (2) the particular process must be tailored to the issue, goal, and audience, and must be sufficiently flexible so that it can evolve over the course of the consultations; (3) the public should be involved throughout all stages of the policy process; (4) there must be room for the public to have real influence on decisions, rather than merely legitimate previous decisions or air grievances; (5) all participants must clearly understand the scope of their role from the outset to avoid disillusionment; (6) timely and accessible information must be provided to all participants; (7) models must be realistic in their timelines, which includes on the one hand sufficient time for participants to inform themselves and to consult their constituents or members, while also ensuring reasonable limits on the length of time so that decisions can be made expeditiously; (8) neutral parties should act as facilitators; (9) working with a problem-solving approach that has consensus as the goal (though both are often impossible to attain in practice); and (10) communication with the media and through the media to the broader public remains essential.[11]

Application to Intergovernmental Relations

These general principles for effective citizen engagement apply to files with an intergovernmental component as well, but as noted above, intergovernmental policy making has a unique set of challenges. Nonetheless, it is possible to identify guidelines that would help governments better manage citizen engagement initiatives in these areas. In general, governments should collaborate in the planning of consultation activities and representatives from

9. See John Forester, *Critical Theory, Public Policy, and Planning Practice: Toward a Critical Pragmatism* (Albany: State University of New York Press, 1993).

10. Michael Morrell provides evidence that many citizens are uncomfortable with the strong demands that would be placed on them during citizen engagement exercises, such as the obligation to express their views publicly and subject them to challenge (see "Citizens' Evaluations of Participatory Democratic Procedures: Normative Theory Meets Empirical Science," *Political Research Quarterly* 52, no. 2 (1999): 293–322). However, our view is that coercing citizens to participate in engagement exercises is never appropriate. Instead, we support innovative models that allow experts, stakeholders, elected officials, and willing members of the general public to formulate recommendations based on a real array of evidence. See Ortwin Renn, Thomas Webler, Horst Rakel, Peter Dienel, and Branden Johnson, "Public Participation in Decision Making: A Three-Step Procedure," *Policy Sciences* 26 (1993): 189–214.

11. For further discussion of these principles, see Katherine Graham and Susan Phillips (eds.), *Citizen Engagement: Lessons in Participation from Local Government* (Toronto: Institute of Public Administration of Canada, 1998), and Frances Abel, Katherine Graham, Alex Ker, Antonia Maioni and Susan Phillips, *Talking with Canadians: Citizen Engagement and the Social Union* (Ottawa: Canadian Council on Social Development, 1998).

all governments should be present during engagement activities. Activities should be jointly sponsored by governments, with general agreement on the nature of consultation activities. This would include agreement on participants or the selection process for participants, the selection of facilitators, the role of elected officials, the objectives of the exercise, the content of information materials, and the reports which assess the outcomes of activities and issue recommendations. It could likewise include commitments from all governments to adhere to — or, more realistically, at least consider seriously — the recommendations emerging from the process. Although governments have the ultimate decision-making authority and can ignore recommendations emerging from engagement exercises should they choose, having all governments involved during all stages of the process will prevent governments which do not like the results of processes from condemning the engagement exercise itself as biased against their own position. In the process, intergovernmental policy making should emerge as more collaborative because of the strong incentive for cooperation created by public processes.

It is true that individual governments could sponsor their own consultations and seek out the views of their own citizens in areas of intergovernmental policy making. In such instances, it would be advisable for governments to inform each other of these activities and provide other governments with opportunities to participate early in the process and be present during activities. Although consultations sponsored by individual governments could prove useful, we argue that engagement activities will be more effective if they are jointly sponsored. This is because there could be strong institutional pressures for engagement activities to produce recommendations consistent with the government's own policy preference when one government alone is responsible for choosing the nature of the activity, the preparation of materials, the framing of the issue, and other matters. There is a real risk that when one government alone undertakes engagement activities, the process will be less sincere and that the activity itself could be used strategically by one government in order to buttress its position in relation to other governments. Such an outcome is not inevitable, but it is more likely that sincere practices for genuine public deliberation and collaborative decision making will develop if competing governments agree to processes beforehand. An additional concern is that it is more difficult to track the impact of engagement activities when one government alone consults because decisions by other orders of government could have an impact on policy outcomes.

Why Engage?

First and foremost, including citizen engagement will lead to better public policy because it brings an additional range of concerns and perspectives to decisions and leads to more informed decision making by decision makers. In a very real sense, the general public can add value to the deliberations of decision makers by providing additional evidence concerning how policies are affecting citizens. Second, public acceptance of decisions is linked to the perception that the process was fair and open, which is facilitated by citizen engagement. Third, including citizens in the policy-making process will reduce the likelihood of unexpected challenges to policies appearing after decisions have been made. In the past, these challenges have often led to unpredictability in decisions because governments are sometimes forced to rescind announcements in the light of public opposition. This is the irony of tight administrative and executive control: when governments choose to avoid genuine consultations for fear that they will lose some control over the policy process, they in fact run the risk of losing far more control because of the public's capacity to disrupt policy at a later stage, including in the courts.

Engagement may also lead to more robust pan-Canadian civil society. Individuals tend to find meaning and construct their identity in one of three projects: belief in a theological project with belief in God as central; self-actualization, with a focus on individual gratification and withdrawal from other potential community-building exercises; or contribution to a secular and a national vision that focuses on building a better community.[12] The religious project is not consistent with secular Canadian values, and the self-actualization project, while popular, is incomplete and by definition leads to a more atomized society. Therefore, the challenge is to find ways for individual Canadians to participate in public life in meaningful ways that can strengthen their commitment to the national community. Opportunities for citizen engagement would achieve this important goal and contribute to building social capital, interpersonal trust, a more robust public sphere, and a richer civil society. It should be noted that survey research indicates that Canadians are willing to participate in such projects and engagement activities.[13]

Quebec and Alberta in particular have been quite successful in using public consultation processes to forge some degree of consensus on societal direction and, in the process, contribute to the belief that their respective communities have collective meaning. Quite obviously, such processes are more successful when a well-defined community with a common identity already exists — a situation that is a more accurate description of the Quebec community than the Canadian community. But at the same time, it should not be overlooked that communities are created in part through citizen participation in collective projects. Citizens need shared experiences to reinforce community. In Quebec, the state has been able to animate a collective identity because one was pre-existing; yet at the same time, government-led collective activities in which the public participates can also nourish and fertilize pre-existing shared identity. A key component of Canadian identity — its social programs — can be reinforced through citizen participation.

Application to the SUFA

The SUFA articulates a vision of federalism based on shared areas of responsibility rather than the allocation of various jurisdictions to distinct orders of government. By recognizing the need for greater cooperation and consultation in the design and delivery of social policy, the SUFA could move Canada closer to a German model of federalism characterized by shared jurisdictions and extensive intergovernmental coordination, a system that can be particularly immune to citizen participation. One risk in such systems is that competing governments adopt bargaining and negotiation approaches that focus on their own institutional self-interest. This can produce poorer public policies because of what Scharpf identifies as the joint decision-making trap, a problem particularly acute within collaborative models.[14] This trap suggests that governments negotiate to avoid costs and receive benefits, which produces suboptimal policies whose main characteristic is that they are minimally satisfactory to all actors. Scharpf suggests that a policy-making process characterized by a "problem-solving" rather than a "bargaining" approach would overcome this trap. Although we agree that a problem-solving approach would be superior, Scharpf identifies no process that could lead governments to adopt such an approach. We suggest that citizen engagement would encourage a "problem-solving" approach because when political leaders are participating alongside citizens in more public processes, they are less likely to focus on the institutional interests of their government because of citizens' impatience with intergovernmental disputes.

---

12. Andrew Delbanco, *A Meditation on Hope* (Cambridge: Harvard University Press, 1999).

13. Ekos Research, "Rethinking Citizen Engagement Survey" (1998).

14. Fritz Scharpf, "The Joint-Decision Trap: Lessons from German Federalism and European Integration," *Public Administration* 66 (Autumn 1988): 239–78.

In policy areas where jurisdiction is shared, one obstacle to successful intergovernmental negotiations and policy development is the self-interest of governments, which creates inevitable disagreements over the distribution of costs and benefits. The cutting of the Canada Health and Social Transfer by the federal government, coupled with the subsequent creation of boutique programs, is bad public policy but is completely rational in a system where governments compete to avoid costs and receive visibility. The benefit of including citizens in more public ways would mitigate against this. The general public's primary interest is effective public policy which addresses their needs, rather than the variety of additional interests which governments can bring to the table, including an interest in exacerbating conflict, marketing policy, managing issues, shifting blame, or taking credit. Public scrutiny therefore allows citizens and the public policy community to play the role of "honest broker" in seeing that governments stay focused on the public interest. The inclusion of citizens would not eliminate intergovernmental conflicts and citizens are not intended to be substitutes for policy experts, but the competitive interests of governments and their strategic posturing would be checked by the involvement of citizens. While governments often have a range of interests when entering into negotiations with other governments, citizens rarely have such alternative agendas.

This in no way implies there will be a lack of competing interests that seek to have their views represented in policy. However, the combination of public involvement and a problem-solving approach will shift the emphasis to some degree towards common interests and values as key elements in the structuring of social policy. Combining publicity and citizen involvement should produce outcomes that are more consistent with the public interest, in part because debate which is public rather than private is more likely to be framed in terms of the public good rather than the self-interest of the parties, because arguments of self-interest are more difficult to sustain when subject to publicity.[15]

The SUFA is a political agreement between different orders of government and though it has no official legislative status, decisions will be binding on citizens and it could have an enormous effect on the conduct and content of future social policy. One must be very careful to avoid constructing policy edifices based on intergovernmentalism that reduce even further democratic input and accountability. The effects of globalization and an increase in the administrative state have led to a growth in *de facto* guardianship, where direct popular control of governments does not exist beyond periodic elections. The courts, international agencies, administrative bodies, and the Prime Minister's Office make a variety of policy determinations, while the impact of individual members of Parliament and individual Canadians on policy remains low. Yet social policy is an area of the highest priority to citizens, and Canada's social programs are an important part of Canadians' identity, and it is therefore one public-policy area where citizens are able to offer informed participation in terms of the setting of priorities and making value-based choices between competing options. When the development of social policies that play such an important role in defining Canadian citizenship is left to private meetings between federal and provincial governments, a core element of citizens' connection to their state is threatened. This threat could be partially addressed through the use of engagement initiatives that give citizens a greater sense of ownership and responsibility for major social policies.

By providing Canadians with opportunities to publicly discuss social policy, we also expect that it is more likely that Quebec's distinct status and the *de facto* asymmetry in Canada would become formally recognized. In the context of the three-year review of the SUFA,

---

15. Simone Chambers, "Contract or Conversation? Theoretical Lessons from the Canadian Constitutional Crisis," *Politics & Society* 26 (1998): 143–72.

amendments which made explicit mention of Quebec might be sufficient to encourage a future Quebec government to agree to the SUFA, and such amendments are more likely to emerge through public participation than private bargaining between first ministers. English-speaking Canadians have been opposed to recognition of Quebec's national status for a variety of reasons — which do not need to be recounted here — yet on the substance of the question, most do not particularly care if Quebec chooses to organize its social policies in a manner different than other provinces.[16] A public process involving citizens may reveal a greater acceptance of asymmetry than is often imagined by political leaders and allow for the evolution of public policy in a direction more consistent with the nature of Canada. We in no way rejoice at Quebec's exclusion from the SUFA, and the lack of specific recognition of Quebec's status within Canada is troubling. Yet one reason governments have been resistant to Quebec recognition is that they fear a backlash from public opinion within their provinces, and we suggest that citizen engagement processes would help demonstrate to English-Canadian governments that their public is more prepared to accept certain forms of asymmetry than previously imagined, provided that through this recognition the power of English-speaking Canadians and their provincial governments is not reduced. Although the lack of specific responses to Quebec's agenda made it unlikely that a Quebec government could sign the SUFA, citizen engagement processes provide an opportunity for amending the SUFA in ways that address Quebec's concerns and in ways that English-Canadian public opinion can accept.

We should conclude this section by noting the possibility that the SUFA may have no shelf life, and that by the time of its first review, it may have become no more than an interlude in intergovernmental negotiations. Although we believe that this would be unfortunate because the SUFA model would improve the social-policy process in Canada, we recognize that such a fate is a real risk. This provides perhaps the most compelling reason to move quickly to implement the commitments to citizen engagement: through public processes, the SUFA would be provided with public visibility and popular ownership. In the absence of any mechanism within the agreement to monitor governments' compliance, citizen engagement also becomes the most viable means of enforcing the SUFA. Because living up to the SUFA is based on political will, the use of citizen-engagement activities would provide governments with a powerful incentive to fulfil their other SUFA commitments. Through such activities, governments could be held more publicly accountable for commitments they make to other governments on social policy. Strong citizen-engagement mechanisms could play an important role in transforming the SUFA from an intergovernmental agreement into an important element of Canadians' social citizenship.

Models of Engagement

Citizen engagement is much easier to advocate than implement. Can models in fact be developed and put in place? Our own purpose is not a theoretical one, and if we cannot meet the frequently heard challenge that citizen engagement is impossible to integrate with intergovernmental policy formation, we have failed in our purpose.

The failures of past consultation efforts are not in themselves evidence that better processes cannot be developed. Governments have often undertaken public consultations with little intention of keeping options open, conducting ongoing transparent public dialogues, or heeding the advice that they received, and the failure of these processes cannot be

---

16. Matthew Mendelsohn, "Public Brokerage: Constitutional Reform, Public Participation, and the Accommodation of Mass Publics," *Canadian Journal of Political Science* 33, no. 2 (2000): 245–73.

Figure 1. Who Participates?

Selection Process Participants	Open	Invited
Stakeholders (appropriate for issues requiring special expertise and where clashes of values within the general public are unlikely)	Public hearings, parliamentary commissions	Public hearings, parliamentary commissions, traditional consultative meetings, internet polling
General public (appropriate for value-based choices and fact finding regarding the success of programs)	Public meetings	Deliberative polls, citizen juries, internet polling, internet study groups
General public and stakeholder (appropriate for issues of the highest priority)	Study circles, public hearings over lengthy periods of time and geographically dispersed. Meetings organized by voluntary groups to engage the general public.	Study circles, constituent assemblies, deliberative polls. Meetings organized by voluntary groups to engage the general public.

extrapolated to efforts that follow the principles laid out above. In addition to following those practical principles, it is crucial to make appropriate choices regarding the nature of the exercise. One must initially make two choices, which are presented schematically in Figure 1. First, will engagement focus on stakeholders, interest groups, and those with expertise in the policy network, or will it be the general public (or all of the above)? Second, will the invitation to participate be open to all, or will the government have to restrict participation to a selected number? The process of restrictions on participation is inherently problematic, but is sometimes necessary in order to properly manage a workable process that produces timely recommendations. When invitations are issued to selected members of the general public only, processes that choose participants at random are increasingly being used, such as deliberative polls, citizen juries, planning cells, and public panels.[17] It should be noted that even if only stakeholders are being consulted, the lessons of citizen engagement discussed above can still apply, such as the use of a problem-solving approach, a transparent process that the public can witness, and reporting back on how contributions were incorporated into decisions.

We suggest that the concept of "delegated authority" can be successfully used to facilitate engagement activities and make them workable in practice in the realm of intergovernmental policy making. Federal and provincial governments may have difficulty reaching agreement on the substance of policy but they typically have less difficulty agreeing on processes to address these substantive differences. Agreeing to delegate some authority to smaller,

---

17. For more detail on these processes, see: Kathy O'Hara, "Citizen Engagement in the Social Union," Discussion Paper, Canadian Policy Research Networks (CPRN) Roundtable on Citizen Engagement in the Social Union, Ottawa (1997); James Fishkin, *The Voice of the People: Public Opinion and Democracy* (New Haven: Yale University Press, 1995); and Usman Khan (ed.), *Participation beyond the Ballot Box: European Case Studies in State-Citizen Political Dialogue* (London: University College London Press, 1999).

jointly appointed bodies, which include citizen-engagement mechanisms, is practical and plausible. All governments have experience with delegating tasks to administrative bodies, though the idea of jointly delegating authority to a body responsible to both levels of government is more contentious. The usual risk with delegated authority is that it creates a democratic deficit as the administrative state is further entrenched, but including citizen-engagement mechanisms would reduce this effect. Including citizen-engagement mechanisms in smaller administrative bodies is also easier than it would be to include intergovernmental decision making through ordinary channels. In Australia, the Environmental Ministerial Council is an intergovernmental body that has been delegated to make environmental policy, and requires citizen engagement as a part of all environmental review processes, hence creating a more transparent intergovernmental process at which members of the public have legal standing and can participate.

One source of concern for those interested in genuine citizen engagement is that during the 1980s and 1990s, governments began to create more partnerships with the voluntary sector for the purposes of alternative service delivery.[18] While many of these partnerships between public and private agencies have been successful, they can reduce accountability to the public,[19] and the continued development of these partnerships could institutionalize a form of corporatism where stakeholders and partners are consulted in processes invisible to public view. While there is no doubt that private consultations with stakeholders have an important role in the policy-making process, in order for citizen engagement efforts to be successful, one must be very careful that the development of citizen-engagement mechanisms includes a mix between processes open to stakeholders and those open to the general public.

Failure to make the appropriate choices regarding participation and selection procedures have in the past marred some consultation efforts. For example, in March 2000 the federal government announced the funding of an independent study of Canada's oil industry to establish why gasoline prices had risen over the previous months. Part of the study would include public hearings. To determine the reasons for rising prices, the general public has little to offer. The public may be interested in complaining about gas prices, but this is more akin to the traditional venting processes of past consultation efforts and not consistent with the principle that one engages the public only when the public has something meaningful to contribute. To choose another example, the British Columbia government chose to hold public hearings on the treaty with the Nisga'a people only after the agreement had been reached and amendments were virtually impossible, a procedure akin to traditional "tell and sell" processes designed for legitimation purposes.

Conversely, there are instances when public consultations would be highly appropriate where they have not been used. For example, the general choice between the appropriate mix of new spending, debt reduction, and tax reductions is an issue appropriate for study circles or deliberative polls, where the general public and those with expertise can make choices based on their priorities and values, even if governments are left to make most of the major allocation choices. We cannot undertake a full review of all consultation efforts, but we wish to highlight that initial choices about who participates and how they are selected will govern the success of the activity. Therefore, particular attention must be given to using engagement exercises only when citizens can usefully contribute. Governments have traditionally been

---

18. Fred Block, *Revising State Theory: Essays in Politics and Postindustrialism* (Philadelphia: Temple University Press, 1987).

19. Susan Phillips, "How Ottawa Blends: Shifting Government Relationships with Interest Groups" in Frances Abele (ed.), *How Ottawa Spends: The Politics of Fragmentation 1991–92* (Ottawa: Carleton University Press, 1991), 207–10.

prepared to share information, and have sometimes been prepared to offer citizens an opportunity to speak or engage in dialogue, but only rarely have they been prepared to allow the general public to participate in decision making, or even issuing recommendations following information sharing and dialogue.

Models of the Citizen

Once it has been determined who should be engaged and how participants will be selected, a critical issue for the development of sound citizen-engagement initiatives is to clearly define what role citizens will be expected to play. Lack of attention to this issue has contributed to the haphazard development of public consultations. Genuine citizen engagement must begin with a clear conception of what role citizens will play. For the purposes of engagement efforts, citizens can be conceptualized as either consumers of government services, clients of government programs, bearers of rights, or democratic actors. From this initial categorization stem two additional questions: at what stage of the policy-making process should citizens be engaged (information gathering, decision making, or policy evaluation), and what type of process should be used? The method of engagement will be very different depending on the initial theoretical model of the citizen, and the success of the exercise depends on choosing the appropriate model of the citizen for the particular problem, and finding methods of engagement consistent with this conception (see Figure 2).

Citizens have been reconceptualized in the past two decades as consumers of government services. The dominant paradigm of public administration reform during this period has been the "reinvention of government," understood through a neoliberal paradigm focused on

Figure 2. Models of Citizen Engagement

	Agenda-setting Stage	Decision-making Stage	Accountability and Reporting Stage
Citizen as Consumer	Surveys, feedback lines, complaint processes, 1-800 lines	Surveys, feedback lines, complaint processes, 1-800 lines	"Accountability provisions" "Opportunities for feedback" Surveys, ombudspeople, feedback lines, complaint processes, 1-800 lines, internet polling
Citizen as Client	Traditional consultations, surveys, feedback processes	Traditional consultations, input into the ongoing process of decision making	"Accountability provisions" Surveys, ombudspeople, feedback processes, internet discussions
Citizen as Rights Bearer	Charters of Rights, citizens' charters	"Opportunities for feedback" Deliberative polls, citizen juries, study circles, people's conventions	"Mechanisms for appeal" "Opportunities for feedback" "Promoting full participation" "Accountability provisions" Appeal processes, benchmarks and indicators, ombudspeople, tribunals, auditor general-style performance audits
Citizen as Democratic Actor	"Effective mechanisms for participation" Public journalism, public dialogue, "Society We Want" (CPRN)-type projects, internet study groups	"Meaningful input into policies" Study circles, people's conventions, deliberative polls, planning cells, citizens' panels, citizen juries, internet study groups	"Effective mechanisms for participation" "Opportunities for feedback" "Accountability provisions" Panels of Citizens, auditor general-type figure, benchmarks and indicators, annual reports

market-oriented reforms of the public sector.[20] In this model, citizens play the role of "consumers" and governments are expected to deliver programs more efficiently by adhering to the principles of market forces.[21] At the same time, an alternative to the New Public Management model has developed that focuses on democratic public administration, with the citizen playing the role of democratic actor and decision maker.[22] These two models seem to be in conflict, with one focusing on government efficiency and the other on democratic decision making. The treatment of citizens as consumers seems to imply a reduction in their role as democratic actors and potential decision makers.[23] However, we suggest that one should not see these models as in conflict; they should be seen as equally valid conceptions of citizenship that are relevant at different times. Although those who advocate more democratic public administration are often critical of what they describe as the narrow conception of citizenship offered by those from the new public management school, for some kinds of government functions it *is* appropriate to think about citizens as consumers of government services. The development of engagement mechanisms that teach governments how to provide services more efficiently in no way detracts from the other roles of citizenship. On the other hand, for other kinds of choices it is necessary to treat citizens as democratic actors with a stake in policy making who can share with decision makers their values and lived realities.

Some citizens also play the role of clients of government programs. While all citizens are consumers of services and potential democratic actors, only some can be considered clients. University students or those served by programs for the disabled, for example, can be thought of as clients of specific programs. This role must be clearly distinguished from the others because it raises different challenges. Because the groups being served by specific programs are by definition restricted, what these groups call for must be balanced with the concerns of the general population. When formulating policies that serve narrow constituencies, simply providing services more efficiently or following the advice of these communities in terms of policy recommendations may be impossible because of other necessary trade-offs, usually budgetary ones, that may not be apparent to the clients participating in the engagement exercise.

Citizens are also bearers of rights. Since the adoption of the Charter in 1982, Canadians have become increasingly conscious of their constitutionally protected rights, and such a consciousness has expanded to include a belief that rights must be honoured in a variety of other contexts, including such things as Revenue Canada's statement concerning "taxpayers' rights" and human rights commissions. In this fourth role, citizens' individual autonomy is the crucial aspect of their identity, as is the case when citizens are conceived of as consumers. As we will see, developing methods to engage citizens as individuals on issues such as the efficient delivery of services and the right to appeal decisions is far easier than developing institutions to engage them as democratic actors, decision makers and participants in collective projects.

---

20. F. Leslie Seidle, *Rethinking the Delivery of Public Services to Citizens* (Montreal: Institute for Research on Public Policy, 1995).

21. Paul Hoggett, "New Modes of Control in the Public Service," *Public Administration* 74, no. 1 (1996).

22. John Shields and B. Mitchell Evans, *Shrinking the State: Globalization and Public Administration "Reform"* (Halifax: Fernwood, 1998).

23. See, for example: Donald J. Savoie, "What's Wrong with the New Public Management," *Canadian Public Administration* 38, no. 1 (1995); F. Leslie Seidle, "Rapporteur's Comments," in F. Leslie Seidle (ed.), *Rethinking Government: Reform or Reinvention?* (Montreal: Institute for Research on Public Policy, 1993), 214; Guy B. Peters. "The Public Service, the Changing State, and Governance," in Guy B. Peters and Donald J. Savoie (eds.), *Governance in a Changing Environment* (Montreal: McGill-Queen's Press, 1995), 298; and Leslie A. Pal, *Beyond Policy Analysis: Public Issue Management in Turbulent Times* (Scarborough, ON: Nelson, 1997), 62.

Citizen as Consumer

The 1980s and 1990s witnessed an increased preoccupation with citizens as consumers of government services, which has been one component of the neoliberal approach to governance. When citizens are primarily the recipient of government services, the goal of engagement must be to ensure that service delivery is efficient, meets its goals, and does not have unintended obstacles, either for the citizen in general (such as improperly designed web pages) or for particular groups of citizens (such as services that cannot be accessed by the hearing impaired). The efficient delivery of services is often challenging, but the methods of engagement are relatively straightforward and need not be particularly deep or deliberative. This is because competing values and interests — that is, politics — tend not to intervene and there is usually general agreement about the objective of the policy, with discussions focusing on the most efficient means of delivery.

In such situations, feedback mechanisms are the most efficient means of engaging citizens. These include both provider-initiated mechanisms, such as surveys of users and the establishment of internet response surveys at the site of service delivery, and recipient-initiated mechanisms, such as 1-800 lines, e-mail suggestion pages, complaint processes using fax or phone, or the presence of ombudspeople. The "opportunity for feedback" provision in the SUFA, as well as many of the "accountability" provisions, commit governments to efficiently providing Canadians with access to services, and such processes should not be particularly difficult to design and implement. It is also possible that complaints regarding the efficient delivery of services can be primarily the responsibility of whichever government is providing the service directly and hence methods of engagement are far more easily implemented.

Citizen as Bearer of Rights

Many in Canada have focused on the Charter as important in initiating an era of rights-based politics, yet there has been a general shift towards rights-based discourse across all liberal-democratic societies, with agencies and departments codifying citizens' rights in general policy statements. For example, recent governments in the United Kingdom have made extensive use of "citizens' charters" in areas of public service that include codifying the rights of taxpayers, those receiving child support, job seekers, crime victims, and a wide range of others.[24] These citizens' charters set standards for the delivery of public services, provide citizens with complaint procedures, and give citizens information about their legal rights. Some have noted that the use of citizens' charters and developments in administrative law "will have important implications for the rights of citizens — whether as consumers of public services or as [those seeking] justice and fairness in public administration."[25] Chancellor Schroeder of Germany also proposes a "charter of basic rights," including social rights, which would permit citizens to seek redress if agencies or institutions of the European Union (or national governments) violated those rights. How one would seek redress is not always clear in these proposals, but they are part of a trend towards judicialization of politics whereby citizens and groups can appeal to the courts or agencies to have governments conform to their own laws and their own statements of principle. This has been prominent in the environmental field, for example, with public-interest groups taking governments to court to insist that they follow their own regulations to, say, hold impact hearings on particular projects. Administrative boards, enforcement mechanisms open to the public, and arbitration-style processes are straightforward methods through which citizens can be engaged to ensure that governments fulfil their obligations in the area of social policy.

---

24. Seidle, *Rethinking the Delivery of Public Services to Citizens*, chapter 2.

25. Philip Giddings, "The Ombudsman in a Changing World," *Consumer Policy Review* 8, no. 6 (1998): 202–8.

The "mechanisms for appeal" provision in the SUFA commits governments to provide arrangements that would allow citizens to seek redress when commitments to public services are not met. By making a commitment to provide citizens with an opportunity to appeal unfair administrative practices and bring complaints about access, citizens become engaged in the SUFA and are granted legal standing in forcing governments to honour their commitments. The nature of the mechanism through which citizens could bring this about is not specified in the SUFA, but commissions or tribunals with quasi-judicial abilities to enforce their decisions, modelled on the human rights commissions, are well-known to Canadians, are reasonably easy to establish, and could be jointly appointed. Less powerful mechanisms are also available, such as auditor general-like figures appointed by both levels of government but operationally independent, who can conduct performance audits of social policy and report publicly on government success and failure at meeting their own commitments.

Citizens as Clients

Much of social policy in Canada is delivered to targeted groups with specific needs. In the same way as the new public management changed the way governments dealt with citizens as customers, it also encouraged them to deal more efficiently with clients of targeted government services. The difficulty for governments is that while the more efficient delivery of services is a clear objective when thinking of general service delivery, when dealing with targeted programs and particular clients, the efficient delivery of services must be balanced with other priorities. When engaging clients of particular programs, problems often emerge because there may be general agreement among all participants about what should be done, but other, external considerations prevent such action from taking place.

The accountability commitments in the SUFA again provide the strongest commitment to engaging citizens in their role as clients of services. Feedback mechanisms, as we described when discussing the citizen as consumer, are appropriate, but deeper, deliberative mechanisms (discussed below) are also necessary. But regardless of the method, they must feed into other ongoing processes that balance the needs of one group of clients with the needs of others. Because all clients of all programs never come together for priority-setting exercises, when individual groups meet with individual government officials, it must be made clear that the current process will only be one of many that feed into a larger process of decision making. When dealing with clients, engagement activities are more likely to be ongoing, with relationships of trust established between government officials and citizens. It is also when dealing with specific client groups that engagement with interest groups and their leaders — rather than with individual citizens — may be most appropriate, because competing values are often not at stake and all members of the group may have a commonality of interests.

Citizen as Democratic Actor

While citizens can play all four roles and governments must be conscious of each, it is necessary to engage citizens in their capacity as democratic actors if a more robust pan-Canadian identity is to be built around common goals and shared social projects. This area has the potential to be the black hole of citizen engagement, or the one place where it is possible to put into operation meaningful theories of public deliberation. Commitments that promised citizen input into policies were judged by experts to be very hard to achieve.[26] It is

---

26. John McLean and Harvey Lazar, *Assessing the Provisions of the Social Union Framework Agreement*, Institute of Intergovernmental Relations, Working Paper Series (Kingston: Institute of Intergovernmental Relations, forthcoming).

in these shaded quadrants of Figure 2 that the rubber of citizen engagement hits the road of intergovernmental policy making.

To engage Canadians as democratic actors, processes of public dialogue and public brokerage are essential. These include citizen juries, deliberative polls, study circles, planning cells, citizens' panels, and people's conventions, all of which feature a cross section of the Canadian population participating in formal decision making and dialogic bodies, along with public servants and elected officials from both levels of government, in meaningful ways that impact on decisions.[27] When these conditions are met, the news media recognize such bodies as legitimate forums that contribute to decisions, allowing for a monitoring of the impact of engagement exercises on decisions and more informed public awareness of consultative processes leading to particular outcomes. This kind of process permits these public bodies to participate in the first two stages of policy development where priorities are established and choices are made, but it also provides the wider general public with an opportunity to participate in the accountability phase as more informed voters passing judgement on government performance. Most of these can be understood as examples of delegated authority, where the government sincerely turns over some aspect of policy making to an alternative body that includes representatives from the public.

The National Forum on Health is an example of nascent attempts to engage citizens in a critical area of Canadian social policy. The National Forum on Health used professional facilitators in a decision-making process that combined community-based discussion groups with a stakeholder conference and a national conference that brought together members of the public and interest groups. In these deliberative forums, decision makers and the general public worked through issues together, and although conflicts inevitably persisted, the process produced a consensus on many recommendations, several of which were reflected in the 1997 federal budget.[28] However, despite the intergovernmental component to health policy, and despite the fact that provincial governments were invited to attend sessions, many of these governments felt excluded from the National Forum because they were not brought into the process early enough or given an equal voice on key decisions regarding the Forum's character. In the future, public consultations on issues that fall under the SUFA need to adhere more closely to the principles of engagement for intergovernmental arrangements that were outlined earlier in the third section. Because provincial governments did not participate in the Forum, an important principle of citizen engagement was violated, namely, that engagement exercises lead in public ways to identifiable decisions. Clearly, when provincial governments do not participate in a dialogue on health policy, the ability to track and implement recommendations will be limited and accountability will suffer.

The "meaningful input into policies" and the "effective mechanisms for participation" are unambiguous government commitments to permit citizens a role in policy making. While governments may end up ignoring or downplaying these commitments, they are unequivocal. In particular, the "meaningful input into policies" provision cannot be interpreted as one which limits citizens in their role — the provision clearly goes beyond the citizen as consumer, client, or bearer of rights perspective. Likewise, this provision cannot be interpreted as one which limits citizens to participation in limited phases during the policy process, such as reviewing outcomes or discussing priorities. It is with this provision that governments have committed themselves to developing mechanisms for public dialogue and decision-making structures in which citizens have real input.

---

27. See O'Hara, "Citizen Engagement in the Social Union."

28. Rhonda Ferderber, Marie Fortier and Janice Hopkins, "Let's Talk about Health and Health Care" (mimeo).

We suggest that models such as the National Forum on Health demonstrate the ability of the general public, stakeholders, policy experts, and government officials to work together to issue recommendations. We further suggest that such models would be far more effective if they were formalized parts of the policy process on important social policy issues, rather than subject to the whims of particular governments about when or if such public dialogues should take place. Were governments to create such formal bodies for public deliberation, these forums would receive more attention by the media and would be seen by the general public to be credible voices for citizen opinion and concerns. If both orders of government agree together to participate in such formal activities, it will be more difficult for governments to ignore their commitments to each other or to blame other governments for their own failings. Such models are feasible in the area of intergovernmental social policy because finding agreement between governments on questions related to the nature of the engagement process is far less difficult than agreeing to matters of substance. Therefore, governments could agree to the creation of public bodies that would contribute to social policy and that would contain engagement mechanisms. Individual governments may not like the outcomes or recommendations emerging from any particular event, and they could choose to ignore them, but there would be powerful incentives for them to follow through on these processes' recommendations. The creation of such bodies does not permanently harm or benefit the interests of one order of government over the other; they simply add one additional element — public deliberation bodies — that all governments have to factor into their decision making.

Conclusions and Recommendations

Citizen engagement on the social union could contribute to better policy, more predictable decision making, increased confidence and trust in government, a more robust pan-Canadian civil society, and a better understanding of the inevitable asymmetry within the country. These goals can only be reached, however, if engagement efforts are sincere and properly designed. The occasional use of poorly designed, hastily conceived efforts — often after policy decisions have already been made or on issues about which the sponsoring government can do little — will usually fail. Many engagement exercises have not been successful because citizens are asked to play the role of democratic actor but are provided with relatively shallow methods of consultation — such as a 1-800 feedback line — that are more appropriate for providing feedback on service delivery. Such shallow mechanisms are appropriate for alerting those implementing policy to problems with the delivery of services, but not for engaging Canadians in the process of making well-informed decisions. The mechanism chosen for engagement must be appropriate for the task at hand, and we must refrain from dismissing robust citizen engagement as impossible because of past failures, many of which did not appropriately match what was being asked of the citizen to the mechanism for engagement.

We recommend the establishment of a council or advisory committee jointly appointed by both orders of government that would be responsible for making recommendations on engagement activities, some of which could include delegating decision-making authority to engagement processes. Although it is far from evident that governments would welcome such a body, the presence of an independent body charged with making recommendations on what kinds of engagement activities to use in particular circumstances could greatly simplify governments' tasks regarding citizen engagement. By securing governments' agreement early in the policy-development process on the nature of engagement exercises, such a committee could alleviate some of the pressure on governments. As it stands, government departments are forced to develop consultative processes — or marshal arguments for avoiding such processes — anew in each policy sector as issues arise. Through the creation of a body with

Figure 3. Approaches to Policy Making

	Problem-solving Approach (brokerage, accommodation models)	Negotiation Approach (conflictual models)
Participatory	"Public brokerage," "accommodation of mass publics," deliberative democratic institutions	Referendums, elections, traditional interest-group interventions
Non-participatory	"Elite accommodation," "consociationalism" "executive federalism"	Court processes, hearings, binding arbitration, other adversarial processes

Figure 4: Further Approaches to Policy Making[29]

	Deliberative	Non-deliberative
Informed	Deliberative democratic institutions: citizen juries, planning cells, deliberative polls, etc.	Choice questionnaires
Uninformed	Focus Groups	Polls

expertise and eventually experience in the area of citizen engagement, the management of the intergovernmental policy process would be simplified for all governments. The committee would also be charged with developing new models of engagement or new applications of existing models, and would be charged with surveying the international community on best practices for citizen engagement on those files that fall under the SUFA.

We also recommend that each province and the federal government establish a legislative committee to track their governments' compliance with the commitments to citizen engagement on the SUFA. Because governments have yet to take significant steps towards implementing the commitments to citizen engagement, these committees could help prod their governments into action and could also propose ways for the commitments to be met in a realistic manner. Representation on these legislative committees would consist of members from the major parties in the legislature as well as a significant number of representatives from the general public and the social policy community.

It is important to note that we are not participatory utopians, magically believing that political conflict vanishes or that all problems are resolved through public participation. Nor do we believe that there is one "off the shelf" model, process, or institution that can facilitate citizen involvement. What we do suggest is that decision makers in the realm of social policy should alter their philosophy and approach to some degree and ask themselves how

---

29. This is adapted from Maggie Mort, Stephen Harrison and Therese Dowswell, "Public Health Panels: Influence at the Margins" in Khan (ed.), *Participation beyond the Ballot Box*, 98.

one can facilitate public dialogue on the issues they are dealing with, how one might charge other voluntary organizations with conducting such dialogue, and how the results of this dialogue can feed into — and be seen to feed into — the social-policy process.

The theoretical goal for those interested in designing methods of citizen engagement for the SUFA is to find mechanisms that bridge the two animating principles of the SUFA — intergovernmental cooperation and public involvement (see Figure 3, shaded quadrant). This would ideally produce mechanisms that value informed and deliberative input (see Figure 4, shaded quadrant). The Canadian political-science community, particularly students of federalism and constitutional processes, has assumed that integrative bargaining, brokerage, integration, and seeking consensus can only occur among small groups of elites (i.e. elite accommodation and executive federalism). However, the brokerage of conflict can take place publicly with the active involvement of the public in seeking ways to accommodate differences (see Figure 3).[30] The SUFA commitments become an opportunity to implement this approach to decision making.

---

30. Mendelsohn, "Public Brokerage."

CHAPTER FOUR

Social Union, Social Assistance: An Early Assessment[1]

Gerard W. Boychuk

Any assessment of the Social Union Framework Agreement (SUFA) and the broader social union approach implicates at least three sets of values: social policy values, democratic values, and federalism values.[2] The strongest objection to the SUFA rejects the particular balance among these values inherent in the agreement, arguing that it is predicated on principles such as subsidiarity and solidarity that do not fit well with the principles of federalism.[3] This compelling and forceful critique of the social union is based on a normative judgement that the social union unduly favours principles such as efficiency and effectiveness (the basic underpinnings of the notion of subsidiarity) over the values inherent in federalism such as the recognition of and respect for diversity. However, for many Canadians the collaborative social-union approach has considerable appeal, especially if portrayed as a trade-off between effective policy and respect for federalism values:

> most English-speaking Canadians have no principled commitment to respecting the existing constitution division of powers. On the contrary, their expectations and attributions of responsibility are naturally directed to the federal government even in areas of provincial jurisdiction … and they would support federal intervention in almost any area of policy so long as it provided good governance.[4]

From this perspective, the question remains as to whether the SUFA and the broader social-union approach are likely to provide "good governance" in the area of social policy and whether this approach is likely to deliver in terms of efficiency, effectiveness, and transparency. This chapter, using the example of the National Child Benefit (NCB), argues that it is not.

---

1. I would like to thank all the participants at the Saskatchewan Institute of Public Policy Forum, "Perspective and Directions: The Social Union Framework Agreement," who made comments on the argument presented in this chapter. I would especially like to thank certain (unnamed) government officials whose conversations with me on this topic sparked considerable thought and reworking of the argument.

2. Keith Banting, "The Past Speaks to the Future: Lessons from the Postwar Social Union," in Harvey Lazar (ed.), *Canada: The State of the Federation 1997, Non-Constitutional Renewal* (Kingston: Queen's University, Institute for Intergovernmental Relations, 1998), 50. See also, Margaret Biggs, *Building Blocks for Canada's New Social Union*, Working Paper no. F-02 (Ottawa: Canadian Policy Research Networks, 1996).

3. Alain Noël, "Without Quebec: Collaborative Federalism with a Footnote," in this volume. See also, Noël, "The Federal Principle, Solidarity and Partnership," in Roger Gibbins and Guy LaForest (eds.), *Beyond the Impasse, Toward Reconciliation* (Montreal: Institute for Research on Public Policy, 1998).

4. Will Kymlicka, "Multinational Federalism in Canada: Rethinking the Partnership," in Gibbins and LaForest (eds.), *Beyond the Impasse*, 37.

Social assistance provision has been a privileged policy area in discussions of the social union. Income maintenance for low-income families has been the area in which the greatest strides have been made under the new social-union approach, and agreement in this area — the NCB — helped to pave the way for the SUFA. While there is technically no formal link between the NCB and the SUFA, collaboration on the former is often used as an example of what might be achieved under the broader rubric of the social union. The NCB has become the poster program of the new collaborative social-union approach.

After examining the provisions of the SUFA which directly relate to social assistance provision, it seems unlikely that the SUFA itself will have a significant impact on the provision of social assistance in Canada either now or in the future. The SUFA simply has few provisions directly relating to the provision of social assistance and those that do exist do not go much beyond intergovernmental commitments which were already in existence.

Second, this chapter assesses the likely impact of the new *spirit* of social unionism by examining the NCB as a model of what might be achieved under this new mode of federal-provincial cooperation. The NCB represents a quite minimal achievement in terms of federal-provincial collaboration and provides slim grounds on which to base expectations of significant future achievements under the SUFA. This chapter argues, however, that this is a good thing. The NCB demonstrates how social policy values may be compromised when the attainment of federal-provincial agreement predominates in social policy-making. By extension, this chapter argues that the SUFA "does not augur well for social policy in Canada."[5] Even if one were to accept a more instrumental focus on "what works" over a principled approach to respect for federalism values (a position which I certainly do not endorse), the SUFA and the new social unionism seem unlikely to deliver.

The Social Union Framework Agreement and Social Assistance

As regards social assistance, two broad components of the SUFA are relevant — one focusing on the process of intergovernmental decision-making and one focusing on the substance of social assistance provision. A brief assessment of both suggests that the SUFA is unlikely to have major direct impacts on the provision of social assistance by the provinces.

Substantive Aspects of the Agreement

The agreement makes reference to a series of substantive principles which would apply across the range of Canadian social programs. The signatories agree to "ensure access for all Canadians, wherever they live or move in Canada, to essential social programs and services of reasonably comparable quality." Secondly, signatory governments agree, in providing programs to meets the needs of Canadians, to "promote the full and active participation of all Canadians in Canada's social and economic life." In order to sustain social programs, governments agree to "ensure adequate, affordable, stable and sustainable funding for social programs." These broad principles are all sufficiently vague, so that it is very difficult to see how they would have a direct impact on social assistance provision.

There are also specific aspects of the SUFA that pertain directly to the substance of social-assistance policy. In meeting the needs of Canadians, signatory governments agree to "provide appropriate assistance to those in need." Secondly, signatory governments agree to "eliminate, within three years, any residency-based policies or practices which constrain access to … social services and social assistance unless they can be demonstrated to be reasonable and consistent with the principles of the Social Union Framework." In ensuring fair and transparent practices, governments have agreed to "have in place appropriate

5. Noël, "Without Quebec."

mechanisms for citizens to appeal unfair administrative practices and bring complaints about access and service."

There is little reason to think that the provision to "provid[e] appropriate assistance to those in need" means much at all considering its formulation. The agreement might be compared to two alternative formulations that immediately come to mind: simply "providing assistance to those in need" or alternatively "providing adequate assistance to those in need." Agreeing to provide assistance to those in need is in some senses a stronger guarantee than the actual formulation of providing appropriate assistance. Historically in Canada, many provincial governments have clearly felt that the most appropriate assistance for a range of recipients was little to none at all. It is not surprising that the SUFA commits governments to providing *appropriate* rather than *adequate* assistance considering that "[i]n Canada, the basic principle is that social assistance should not exceed the income of low-income households in employment, not to give a reasonable standard of living."[6] Social assistance rates in Canada have never been based on notions of adequacy — "benefit levels are not linked to any 'objective' measure of poverty," nor are they tied to inflation.[7] Rather, considering Canadian tradition in this regard, "appropriate" assistance is more likely to refer to "ensur[ing] that the benefit system should not support a standard of living that exceeds or even matches that of a working household"[8] rather than some notion of adequacy. As well, even under the Canada Assistance Plan (CAP), which required that assistance be provided to anyone deemed to be in need, need was defined by the provinces. Under this condition, there remained a wide variety of grounds on which recipients could be denied assistance even though they were obviously in need.[9] This tradition of provincial definition of need will certainly continue under the SUFA.

Secondly, the agreement to eliminate residency requirements will not have much effect in the area of social assistance where such requirements already contravene the Canada Health and Social Transfer.[10] Under the SUFA, the provinces have voluntarily agreed to accept this principle which previously stood as the last federally imposed condition of social assistance provision.

In contrast, the commitment to "have in place appropriate mechanisms for citizens to appeal unfair administrative practices and bring complaints about access and service" may have some limited impact on social assistance provision by the provinces. In some provinces — like Ontario — the range of appealable decisions has been narrowed and this commitment may help forestall further narrowing of appeal procedures.[11] This provision may place

---

6. Organisation for Economic Co-operation and Development, *The Battle against Exclusion, Vol. 3: Social Assistance in Canada and Switzerland* (Paris: OECD, 1999), 43.

7. Ibid., 59.

8. Ibid.

9. Gerard W. Boychuk, *Patchworks of Purpose: The Development of Provincial Social Assistance Regimes in Canada* (Kingston and Montreal: McGill-Queen's University Press, 1998), 46–47.

10. This is the sole remaining federal condition for the funding ostensibly provided for social assistance under the CHST. Since rolling social assistance into block-funding for health and post-secondary education under the CHST, "[t]he cuts to federal payments to the provinces under the Canada Health and Social Transfer will amount to about what Ottawa spent previously on provincial welfare spending..." Ken Battle, "The National Child Benefit: Best Thing Since Medicare or New Poor Law?," in Douglas Durst (ed.), *Canada's National Child Benefit: Phoenix or Fizzle?* (Halifax: Fernwood, 1999), 53. The federal move can thus be reasonably interpreted as complete federal withdrawal from social assistance. See Gerard W. Boychuk, "Aiming for the Middle: Challenges to Federal Income Maintenance Policy," in Leslie A. Pal (ed.), *How Ottawa Spends, 2001–2002: Power in Transition* (Don Mills, ON: Oxford University Press, 2001) 123–44.

11. National Council of Welfare, *Another Look at Welfare Reform* (Ottawa: Minister of Public Works and Government Services, 1997), 69.

some moral pressure on governments to maintain appeal procedures at the standards which developed under the CAP.

Process Aspects of the Agreement

While there is nothing in the agreement specifically related to the process of policy making in the area of social assistance, there is agreement regarding the broader process of policy making including commitments to measuring results, involving citizens, ensuring fair and transparent practices, and pursuing joint planning and collaboration between governments. In terms of measuring results, each government agrees to "monitor and measure outcomes of its social programs and report regularly to its constituents on the performance of these programs." This aspect of the agreement also has an intergovernmental aspect to it as signatory governments have agreed to "share information and best practices to support the development of outcomes measures, and work with other governments to develop, over time, comparable indicators to ensure progress on agreed objectives." Signatory governments have also committed to the principle of citizen involvement and have agreed to "ensure effective mechanisms for Canadians to participate in developing social priorities and reviewing outcomes." Finally, signatory governments "agree to collaborate on implementation of joint priorities when this would result in more effective and efficient services to Canadians, including as appropriate joint development of objectives and principles, clarification of roles and responsibilities, and flexible implementation to respect diverse needs and circumstances, complement existing measures and avoid duplication."

Measuring and Sharing Results

Obviously, it is difficult for observers outside the governmental process to discern the degree to which measuring and sharing of results takes place. However, on the face of it, the track record in Canada of measuring and sharing results regarding the provision of social assistance has been abysmal in comparison, for example, to the United States. Canadian jurisdictions are not yet at the point of producing publicly available comparable data on policy *outputs* much less policy *outcomes*. The most recent publicly available comparable data on maximum hypothetical benefit levels are roughly two years old and average social-assistance rates as actually paid by the provinces are unavailable.[12] Thus far, there has been no indication in this area that this situation has changed or is likely to change.

The measurement of policy outcomes within specific provinces does not appear much better. For example, Alberta — one of the Canadian jurisdictions that has gone the furthest towards measuring results — has kept no data on the number of people applying for social assistance in comparison to the number to whom it is actually granted, despite the fact that their primary social-assistance strategy has been one of diverting applicants for social-assistance recipients. With some exceptions, it remains unclear at this time what measured results provinces have or would be willing to share.

Citizen Participation

For a variety of reasons, including general public antipathy to the issue and a tradition of extremely closed policy making in this area, it is unlikely that policy making in the area of social assistance is likely to open up significantly.

Funding

The aspects of the SUFA referring to intergovernmental funding of social programs are

---

12. This raises the question of how the public or social policy observers would even know if provinces were to lower their social assistance rates as actually paid through reductions in special allowances, etc.

unlikely to have significant implications for social assistance provision. The agreement to "use funds transferred from another order of government for the purposes agreed and pass on increases to its residents" is unlikely to have significant implications for social assistance now that funding for this area is rolled in with health and post-secondary education under the Canada Health and Social Transfer (CHST). Presumably, the provinces are agreeing to use any increases in CHST funding within the broad areas covered by the CHST and not any one particular area.

There may be new, Canada-wide initiatives in social assistance that are funded through intergovernmental transfers. Should this be the case, such initiatives would presumably be governed by the collaborative principles outlined in the SUFA. However, in the immediate future, such initiatives appear unlikely. Rather, for the foreseeable future, federal influence in areas such as social assistance appears much more likely to be in the form of direct transfers to individuals such as those under the NCB, in keeping with the trend which Jerome-Forget describes as "a definite trend toward highly visible and direct federal interventions..."[13] The requirements for consultation regarding these types of initiatives are simply for the federal government to give three months notice prior to implementation and to "offer to consult."

Collaboration/Clarification of Roles and Responsibilities/Flexible Implementation

In the area of social assistance, the federal commitments to collaboration and flexible implementation ring a bit hollow. In the area of social assistance, the federal agreement to "consult prior to implementing new social policies and programs that are likely to substantially affect other governments" is virtually a requirement, considering the federal government's limited jurisdictional status in the field. The history of cost sharing in the area of social assistance in Canada suggests that — at least in this policy area — money is not necessarily a good substitute for jurisdiction.[14] Not only is it "very hard for one government to impose standards on another reluctant government" using spending power,[15] it is also very difficult to shape outcomes by direct spending alone in a policy field over which another level of government retains sole legislative jurisdiction.

Secondly, the most obvious area where governments might consider collaboration in order to operate more effectively is in the area of income maintenance for the unemployed. The relationship between social assistance and Employment Insurance (EI) is marked by a notable lack of collaboration or even information sharing. In the area of income maintenance, the litmus test of the collaborative approach would be the federal government consulting the provinces regarding future major changes to EI — something it is not required to do under the SUFA. A more modest achievement would be meaningful cooperation on information sharing regarding income support for the unemployed, although there appears to have been very little development in this direction.[16]

---

13. Monique Jerome-Forget, "Canada's Social Union: Staking Out the Future of Fiscal Federalism," *Policy Options-Options politiques* 19, no. 9 (November 1998): 3–4.

14. See, for example, Boychuk, *Patchworks of Purpose*, esp. 103.

15. Richards argues: "At most, national standards operate on the fringe of social policy; it is very hard for one government to impose standards on another reluctant government." John Richards, "Reducing the Muddle in the Middle: Three Propositions for Running the Welfare State," in Harvey Lazar (ed.), *Canada: The State of the Federation 1997, Non-Constitutional Renewal* (Kingston: Institute of Intergovernmental Relations, 1998), 99.

16. Tom McIntosh and Gerard Boychuk, "Dis-Covered: EI, Social Assistance and the Growing Gap in Income Support for the Unemployed in Canada," in Tom McIntosh (ed.), *Federalism, Democracy and Labour Market Policy in Canada* (Kingston: SPS/McGill-Queen's University Press, 2000). For a shorter version, see Gerard Boychuk and Tom McIntosh, "Adrift among Islands: Income Support for the Unemployed in Canada," *Canadian Review of Social Policy* (forthcoming).

Finally, regarding the clarification of roles, it is important to note that clarity per se does not necessarily mean that responsibilities will be divided so as to ensure that governments effectively deal with social policy problems. For example, in the case of income support for the unemployed, it is precisely the growing clarity in the division of responsibilities between the two orders of government (federal responsibility through EI only for those with a strong attachment to the labour force and provincial responsibility through social assistance only for those with very little attachment to the labour force) that has contributed to a growing gap between the two programs that appears likely to develop into a significant social problem in the next economic downturn.[17]

While an examination of the SUFA suggests that the agreement itself will not have a major direct impact on the provision of social assistance by the provinces in Canada, this is not to say that the underlying spirit of the agreement will not have significant effects. It is to a consideration of this issue which this chapter now turns through an examination of the NCB.

The National Child Benefit

The NCB, though it preceded the SUFA, is the poster program of the new collaborative approach.[18] Hailed as the most important social policy initiative in over thirty years,[19] the NCB has been portrayed (among other things!) as a phoenix — "the mighty federal government rising from the ashes of the great social welfare era of the postwar period."[20] The NCB is often used as an example of what might be achieved under the new social-union approach both in terms of social policy substance as well as process. The Organization for Economic Cooperation and Development notes that "[a]mongst representatives of the governments involved, virtually no-one says a bad word about the NCB, which is praised both for the policy direction but also for the process which led to it."[21] However, the contrary argument presented here is that federal-provincial agreement on the NCB represented a quite modest achievement. Rather, the NCB points to the dangers in terms of social policy values that may arise when the attainment of federal-provincial agreement predominates in social-policy making.

Creating work incentives through the extension of income-tested (rather than means-tested) benefits to the working poor is the model which underpins the NCB. The NCB is not so much a departure from existing social policy practice as it is a departure from existing modes of federal-provincial interaction in social policy. The Child Tax Benefit, which was replaced in the shift to the NCB, emerged out of a long process of changes to the Family Allowance program which began in 1978. Along with other quite minor changes, the NCB simply enriched the existing Child Tax Benefit by roughly 60% for the first child to $1,625 annually from the existing benefit of $1,020.[22] While entailing increased expenditures, in and

---

17. See McIntosh and Boychuk, "Dis-Covered."

18. Lazar notes: "At the sectoral level, perhaps the largest move toward the collaborative approach to the social union has been made in the area of child benefits." Harvey Lazar, "The Federal Role in a New Social Union: Ottawa at the Crossroads," in Lazar (ed.), *Canada: The State of the Federation 1997, Non-Constitutional Renewal*, 121.

19. See, for example, Anne McLellan, "Modernizing Canada's Social Union: A New Partnership among Governments and Citizens," *Policy Options-Options politiques* 19, no. 9 (November 1998): 7.

20. Douglas Durst, "Phoenix or Fizzle? Background to Canada's New National Child Benefit," in Durst (ed.), *Canada's National Child Benefit: Phoenix or Fizzle?*, 14.

21. OECD, *The Battle Against Exclusion*, 131.

22. Federal/Provincial/Territorial Ministers Responsible for Social Services, "The National Child Benefit: Building a Better Future of Canadian Children" (September 1997) [http://www.intergov.gc.ca/docs/intergov/ncb/1_e.html]. These enriched benefits will entail an increase of $1.7 billion over several years. McLellan, "Modernizing Canada's Social Union," 7.

of itself, the enriched federal benefit does not mark a significant departure from the existing federal approach to providing benefits for low-income children.

The significant new element was the level of coordination among the federal and provincial governments. The NCB package was designed by the Federal/ Provincial/Territorial Ministers Responsible for Social Services and is coordinated by the Council on Social Policy Renewal. Under this agreement, the federal and provincial governments have agreed on three objectives for the National Child Benefit:

> • to help prevent and reduce the depth of child poverty;

> • to promote attachment to the workforce — resulting in fewer families having to rely on social assistance — by ensuring that families will always be better off as a result of working; and

> • to reduce overlap and duplication through closer harmonization of program objectives and benefits through simplified administration.[23]

In pursuing these three broad objectives, the NCB agreement entails three distinct but complementary components:

> • the federal government will increase its benefits for low-income families with children, enabling it to assume more financial responsibility for providing basic income support for children;

> • corresponding with the increased federal benefit, provinces and territories will decrease social assistance payments for families with children, while ensuring these families receive at least the same level of overall income support from governments;

> • provinces and territories will reinvest these newly available funds in complementary programs targeted at improving work incentives, benefits and services for low-income families with children.[24]

While the federal and provincial governments broadly agree that benefits under provincial reinvestment strategies should be directed to children in need, there is latitude for a wide range of distinct approaches — rather than a single coordinated approach — to how such benefits should be structured and delivered and even to whom they should be targeted. Provinces may adopt one or a mix of several approaches including:

> • income support programs for low-income families with children and the extension of in-kind benefits now available for children in social assistance families, such as health benefits, to a broader range of low-income families;

> • earned income supplements for low-income families with children; and/or

> • the improvement of child benefits to families receiving social assistance and the provision of social services, such as child care, that support attachment to the workforce.[25]

Perhaps most importantly, the NCB signals a particular direction in the federal approach to collaboration itself:

> with Ottawa's fiscal situation improving more rapidly than expected, there are indications that federal-provincial relations will be subject to a new set of dynamics. Rather than restoring social transfers to the provinces or reducing the tax room it occupies to reflect a diminished federal role in social policy, we see a definite trend toward highly visible and direct federal interventions…[26]

---

23. Ibid.
24. Ibid.
25. Ibid.
26. Jerome-Forget, "Canada's Social Union: Staking Out the Future of Fiscal Federalism," 3–4.

Assessing the Substance of the NCB

Even though the NCB often serves as an example of what might be achieved under the collaborative social-union approach, the substance of the agreement itself — both in terms of its intergovernmental aspects and its social-policy aspects — represents a relatively minimal achievement. It was, according to some observers, a "natural deal." In fact, the major elements of the agreement appear to have been designed to ensure that little adjustment on the part of the provinces was necessary. The NCB can be argued to fall into that class of collaborative efforts which have emerged in "areas where little adjustments were necessary" and "where in fact collaboration did not mean much."[27]

The NCB as a Federal-Provincial Agreement

At root, the NCB is a negotiated attempt by the federal government to do what it has always maintained it has had the right to do and what the provinces (notably Quebec) have often denied it has the right to do — spend its own funds as it wished even should these expenditures lie in areas of provincial jurisdiction. As noted above, the history of cost-sharing in social assistance suggests that money is not necessarily a good substitute for jurisdiction. The difficulty for the federal government has been that provinces have the ability to significantly offset federal efforts:

> In the early years of the first Chrétien government, Ottawa was reluctant to put additional money into the reduction of child poverty… While federal reluctance … was, in the main, due to fiscal restraint, Ottawa shied away from acting because it was open to provincial governments to reduce their social assistance payments, dollar for dollar, to offset the impact of any improvements Ottawa might make with the result effectively being no improvement in the income levels of poor families with children.[28]

While dealing with this problem required provincial cooperation, the NCB is quite simply the expansion and simplification of an existing federal program. The NCB did not fundamentally displace any existing federal (or provincial) programs and the federal government continues to get full recognition for the benefits provided directly to low-income families under the program. The main achievement of the intergovernmental agreement is that provinces have agreed not to redirect expanded federal funding (by clawing back federal benefits through reducing social assistance benefits) to other nonrelated policy areas. Seen in this light, the NCB can hardly be characterized as "the mighty federal government rising from the ashes of the great social welfare era of the postwar period."[29]

In addition, the NCB is predicated on social-policy principles which were not only broadly acceptable to Quebec but which espoused a social-policy approach of which Quebec has been a leading exemplar. Quebec introduced income-tested child benefits earlier than any other province and has proceeded considerably further along these lines than any other province. Lazar and McIntosh note:

> There is a risk in the formalizing of the social union. They could potentially enhance social bonds among Canadians outside Quebec but at the price of creating a new and large irritant between the Government of Quebec and other

---

27. Noël, "Without Quebec." Noël himself however, argues that the NCB is a more critical case in which "collaboration was only obtained because the provinces yielded." The following argument offers a considerably different reading of the agreement.

28. Lazar, "The Federal Role," 122.

29. Durst, "Phoenix or Fizzle?," 14.

Canadian governments. How the framework agreement on the social union plays itself out will be crucial. Will Quebec effectively abide by the rules even though it has not signed? Alternatively, will the signatories behave in a way that makes it easy for Quebec to accommodate to what occurs within the social union framework?[30]

Considering Quebec's track record in this area, it is easy for the federal government to accept that, in this particular policy area, "Quebec would effectively abide by the rules even though it has not signed the agreement" and, at the same time, proceeding along these lines makes it "easy for Quebec to accommodate what occurs within the social union framework."[31]

Securing Provincial Agreement

In fact, with the obvious and significant exception of Quebec, securing provincial agreement on the NCB was a relatively modest achievement. As noted above, the revised benefit program did not displace any existing provincial programs, nor did it require any commitment of provincial resources. The only thing required of the provinces was that they promise not to divert increased federal benefits away from low-income programs to other program areas through clawing back social-assistance benefits. Thus, the agreement limits the extent to which the federal expenditures represent a windfall to provincial coffers; however, even under these arrangements, federal expenditures do represent a financial bonus to the provinces to the extent that provinces can use "the extra money to offset what they would have spent anyway."[32]

In turn, the provinces were asked to give up virtually none of their control over social-assistance programs. The reinvestment requirements are very low:

> there is really no way for the federal government — or provincial governments, for that matter — to influence the reinvestment decisions of a particular province. The two levels of government have negotiated a framework for reinvestments that does little more than draw the boundaries of programs and service deemed acceptable for the reinvestment of welfare savings — "programs targeted at improving work incentives and supporting children in low-income families."[33]

Within the area of income maintenance, provinces have been able to use the funds for just about anything they want and continue to provide social assistance in the manner they want[34]:

> The range of reinvestment activities announced to date by the provinces is broad, and it seems highly unlikely that there will be any sort of standards to govern such programs.[35]

Although the agreement ostensibly "protect[s] the overall benefit levels for families

30. Harvey Lazar and Tom McIntosh, "How Canadians Connect: State, Economy, Citizenship and Society," in Harvey Lazar and Tom McIntosh (eds.), *Canada: The State of the Federation 1998/99, How Canadians Connect* (Kingston: Queen's University, Institute of Intergovernmental Relations, 1999), 17.

31. Ibid.

32. Battle, "The National Child Benefit," 49.

33. Ibid., 51.

34. The three options open for reinvestment under the decision mark significantly distinct approaches to providing benefits to families and need, and are indeed based on fundamentally different assumptions about the causes of poverty and the most appropriate measures for alleviating it. In fact, many observers might disagree that enriching benefits or services targeted to recipients on social assistance is even in keeping with the broad aim of the NCB of "ensuring that families will always be better off as a result of working." While the federal component of the plan is modeled on the first approach, provinces are allowed to adopt quite different reinvestment strategies under the NCB. The provinces have not, thus far, sacrificed their policy latitude in the approach they may choose to adopt in reinvesting social assistance funds.

35. Battle, "The National Child Benefit," 51.

receiving social assistance,"[36] this aspect of the agreement is merely symbolic. While the provinces have agreed not to use increases in the federal benefit as an opportunity to decrease social assistance benefits by an amount greater than the increase, they have not agreed in a general sense to maintain social assistance benefits at their current levels.[37] Any province at any time can undertake benefit cuts of any magnitude of its choosing.

Even the lax reinvestment requirements only apply to the first $2,500 of federal benefits. In determining the benefit levels required to "take children off welfare," federal and provincial officials agreed that provincial social assistance benefits per child are approximately $1,500 — ranging from $1,200 to $1,800 per child per year excluding accommodation-related benefits.[38] Thus, children are to be considered off welfare once income-tested benefits have been increased from $1,020 under the old Child Tax Benefit to a total of $2,500 — the point above which provinces will no longer be expected to reinvest clawed-back benefits. Reinvestment requirements "doubtless will end once Ottawa increases the Canada Child Tax Benefit to the $2,500 remove-children-from-welfare level, since at that time there will be no more provincial welfare benefits to displace…"[39] and provinces no longer bear any responsibility for child poverty.

However, implicit first-child benefits in Canada (the amount of social assistance and federal child tax benefits paid to a single parent with one child in comparison to benefits paid to a single individual) averaged $6,300 across Canadian provinces in 1996. At the point at which governments have agreed that children will no longer be on welfare, income-tested benefits ($2,500) will represent just under 40% of the average implicit first-child benefits previously provided through social assistance.[40] Cynical observers may not find this surprising. There are pressures for the federal government to stipulate a relatively low amount in order to declare a quick victory in "getting children off welfare." Similarly, there are pressures on provinces to concur in order to quickly be relieved of the responsibility for child poverty.

If, as Courchene has recently suggested, the NCB marks a *de facto* revision of the division of powers, it has not been the result of federal strong-arm tactics, infusions of federal cash, or because the provinces have "yielded."[41] The NCB could have been designed in a way that did not entail this shifting of responsibility for children's poverty to the federal government. It was designed this way precisely because the provinces wanted to be (or provincial officials believed it was best to be) absolved of responsibility for child poverty.

The NCB as Social Policy

Three substantive elements of the NCB — a focus on children's benefits, work incentives, and the relationship between the new benefit and social assistance — may well have unintended policy consequences which seriously undermine its self-professed goal of preventing

36. Ibid.

37. Ibid.

38. Department of Finance, *Working Together towards a National Child Benefit System*, 13. It is impossible to determine from this document (or any other publicly available source to my knowledge) how federal-provincial officials arrived at this figure. Even policy analysts — much less the general public — are simply expected to accept that provincial social-assistance benefits averaged about $1,500 per year in the provinces — a dubious claim at best.

39. Battle, "The National Child Benefit," 50.

40. These benefit levels deemed necessary to remove children from welfare are extremely low for three reasons. First, they do not include accommodation-related benefits which are so difficult to calculate because of the serious methodological difficulty in separating child benefits from parental benefits. Secondly, they ignore the higher amounts paid for the first child in a family — again, underestimating benefits. Finally, they make no consideration of adequacy. Under the NCB, children are taken off welfare by partially replacing benefits which many observers already view as inadequate.

41. Noël, "Without Quebec."

and reducing the depth of child poverty. Yet, paradoxically, these elements appear to have been central to federal-provincial agreement in this area. First, the NCB's focus on *children's* (as opposed to family) benefits ideologically neutralized potential provincial opposition, muted ideological differences between governments, and ensured that the program would not threaten "tough on welfare" provinces. Secondly, a focus on work incentives (defining the primary problem as one of people willingly receiving social assistance because it pays more than work) was "a major selling point to governments" and central to securing provincial agreement.[42] The final element central to the agreement was defining the NCB primarily by its relationship to social assistance. The NCB, which provides benefits to low-income families *regardless* of the source of income, is *not* primarily about social assistance. However, discussions surrounding the NCB are characterized by an insistence on the language of "getting children off welfare" — rather than "getting children out of poverty" or any number of other possible spins. This language appears most immediately understandable as a euphemism for absolving provinces of any responsibility for child poverty.

The rhetoric and symbolism of this particular agreement should raise caution flags even for proponents of the income-tested approach. In rhetorically decoupling children's and parents' wellbeing, the NCB is deliberately designed to make social assistance an "adults only" program — a separation which may be difficult to reverse once it takes root. A potentially powerful political dynamic may result from "taking children off welfare." At first blush, the lack of a requirement that provinces maintain welfare spending or their welfare rates does not seem problematic, as there is no apparent reason why the provinces would use the advent of the NCB (or increases to it) as an opportunity to reduce overall welfare-benefit packages below their current levels.[43] Moreover, no one with serious respect for the constitutional division of powers would argue that provinces ought not to have control over social-assistance rates. At the point at which children are considered to no longer be on welfare (combined income-tested benefits of $2,500 — which has already been reached in some provinces), remaining welfare benefits consist only of "parents' benefits."[44]

In addition to symbolically removing children from welfare, the NCB and attendant debate have firmly entrenched the issue of work incentives and the "welfare wall" as the central pillar of Canadian social assistance debates. With the preponderant focus on work incentives, the issue of social-assistance has been firmly cast as one of families willingly — albeit rationally — choosing welfare benefits over employment. Based on the assumption that viable employment options (including suitable employment, child-care options, etc.) exist for almost all social assistance recipient families, the primary policy problem becomes making work pay relative to welfare in order to entice the otherwise reluctant welfare recipients into working. There are two ways to do so — increase benefits to the working poor or decrease social-assistance benefits. Once children are symbolically no longer recipients of welfare benefits in Canada, it may be difficult for governments to resist adopting the latter strategy in their quest to address what will have become defined as the central problem of welfare — employable adults who willingly choose welfare over work because it pays better.

---

42. Battle, "The National Child Benefit," 53.

43. "Though the provinces have promised that welfare families will not be left worse off as a result of the National Child Benefit, it is difficult to imagine this voluntary condition having much meaning over time — i.e. after the provinces have reinvested their welfare savings from increased federal child benefits. Otherwise, the National Child Benefit would score a major victory in getting the provinces to agree to maintain welfare rates for families with children (more precisely, parents' benefits once children's benefits are fully removed from welfare). It would be dreaming in technicolor to hold out such a hope. But at least the provinces will not be allowed to siphon away welfare savings to purposes unrelated to child poverty." Battle, "The National Child Benefit," 49.

44. Ibid.

This combination is likely to generate pressures for tightened eligibility and lowered benefits for such programs at the same time as making it very difficult to defend social assistance on the basis that cuts harm children — who will be, by definitional fiat, no longer dependent on these programs. Provinces have agreed in the short term not to reduce the overall income of families dependent on social assistance. There are absolutely no proscriptions against provinces lowering benefits in the long term, allowing benefits to be eroded by inflation, tightening eligibility or introducing more stringent forms of workfare. Even if provinces were not to explicitly cut welfare benefits (which some may well do after they have reinvested their welfare savings from increased federal child benefits), provinces may succumb to pressures to reduce benefits to these employable adults

> through stealth by delaying or foregoing increases to welfare rates or, as is increasingly the way these days, by reducing rates or making other belt-tightening changes to the welfare system such as cutting special benefits and reclassifying recipients.[45]

Benefit reductions by stealth have become easily achievable in Canada with the general shift from automatic inflation indexing to discretionary increases.[46] To make matters even worse, the levels of benefits that have been designated as child benefits and are thus protected from these dynamics are much lower than the social assistance benefits that families have actually received on behalf of their children. (See Appendix.) Thus, it seems that there is every possibility that families on social assistance may eventually end up worse off under the NCB than they were under provincial social assistance. Certainly, this development would mark a serious policy failure.

This is not to say that these things will necessarily happen. There are some initial indications that some provinces may be moving to reduce benefits: "[r]ecent announcements of cuts to social assistance in Ontario and Nova Scotia would appear to violate the federal-provincial agreement that no child would be 'worse off'."[47] Across provinces, the evidence is more mixed. (See Figure 1.) In three provinces (Alberta, Newfoundland, and New Brunswick), the total benefit income of families with children is higher. Total benefits are significantly higher in the latter two as they are the two provinces that did not institute a clawback of increased federal benefits. In other provinces, the picture is mixed depending on the type of family in question (Quebec and Saskatchewan). Finally, in five provinces, total benefit income was lower for families with children on social assistance in 1999 than in 1997, but this is primarily due to the effects of inflation. While some families with children in certain provinces are indeed worse off than they were prior to the implementation of the benefit, there are no indications yet that this is taking place at an accelerated pace in the wake of the NCB agreement.

However, the rhetoric of the agreement (if it becomes deeply entrenched in policy discourse and public discussion) may alter the balance of political forces and undermine the political underpinnings of existing social assistance systems. It is unlikely that provinces will "cite the National Child Benefit as a rationale for reclassifying single mothers as employable or forcing them into work-for-welfare schemes."[48] But neither is this a meaningful way to monitor the complex interaction between these programs. It *is* likely that the NCB will dampen resistance to such initiatives and will certainly remove the argument that such

---

45. Ibid.

46. OECD, *The Battle against Exclusion*, 59, and T. Eardley et al., *Social Assistance in OECD Countries* (Paris: OECD, 1996).

47. Richard Shillington, "Two Casualties of the Child Tax Benefit: Truth and the Poor," *Policy Options-Options politiques* 21, no. 9 (November 2000): 62–67.

48. Battle, "The National Child Benefit," 53.

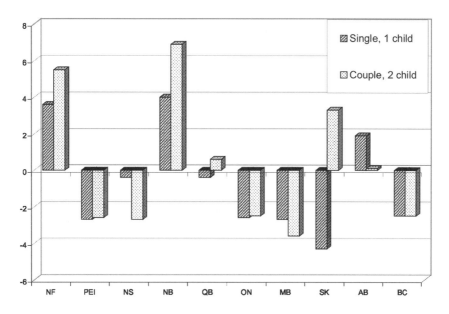

CHANGE (%) IN TOTAL WELFARE INCOME, BY PROVINCE, Adjusted for Inflation,1997-1999

Figure 1.

Source: National Council of Welfare, *Welfare Incomes*, 1997 and *Welfare Incomes*, 1999 (Ottawa: Public Works and Government Services, 2000).

changes are harmful for children from the political arsenal of opponents of such changes. Once children have been nominally removed from social assistance benefits, it will be increasingly difficult to oppose such changes on the basis that they are primarily harming children. Second, once the policy strategy of decoupling the problem of children's poverty from the issue of parental poverty has become firmly established as a central feature of the policy landscape, it will be difficult to later reverse this trend or oppose provincial social assistance cuts on the basis that this separation is nonsensical.

These developments will have profoundly important gendered impacts.[49] The relevant segment of the social assistance caseload (parents with children) is made up predominantly of single parents — the overwhelming share of which are women. Thus, while the discussion above refers to rhetorically decoupling parents' and children's wellbeing, the reality is a decoupling of children's well-being from their *mothers'* wellbeing. Historically, social assistance in Canada has tended to define women as deserving social assistance recipients by virtue as their roles as mothers.[50] Income-tested children's benefits turn this reasoning on its head by completely divorcing single mothers as recipients of social assistance from their role as mothers of families in need. Children in single-parent families will be provided children's benefits just like children in any other low-income family and, presumably, their mothers will

---

49. This argument was pointed out to me by Margaret Little and I would like to record my thanks to her.

50. Often the bargain struck in this regard between the mother and the state mirrored the nature of the sexual bargain implicit in the traditional family — the exchange of the provision of material wellbeing for the provision of the services of caring for children coupled with sexual monogamy. See Boychuk, *Patchworks of Purpose*, esp. 35.

be provided adult benefits on the same basis as any other category of adult recipient such as single, young, employable males. Thus, "[t]he approach allows the federal government the appearance of addressing child poverty at the same time as it takes a tough stand against welfare…"[51] — including welfare for mothers of those very children. The separation of responsibility for the wellbeing of children and the wellbeing of adults between the federal and provincial governments respectively[52] means that "[i]n effect, children are going to receive additional entitlements from the federal government while their mothers may be increasingly disentitled by provincial governments…"[53]

The counterargument to all of these objections is that federal income-tested child benefits will be better protected than provincial social assistance benefits. While likely true, these income-tested benefits are protected at a quite modest level. As the $2,500 benchmark does not include major elements such as shelter benefits, officials agree that children in families receiving social assistance will to some large degree still be dependent upon social assistance despite nominally being off welfare. Income-tested benefits would need to be considerably higher than is currently the case to truly displace children's welfare benefits. However, there are few incentives for the federal government to increase benefits above currently scheduled increases, as provincial governments will not be bound to reinvest clawed-back benefits above the $2,500 mark and may choose to simply reduce social-assistance benefits dollar-for-dollar above this point.

To the extent that the effects outlined above actually develop and to the extent that they are unintended, they would mark a serious policy failure. This is not to say that the NCB is doomed to fail but that it will not succeed by acclamation. Its long-term success in reducing the depth of family poverty remains an open empirical question. There are, however, compelling reasons to remain skeptical.

Assessing the NCB as a Collaborative Intergovernmental Process

The process culminating in the NCB is probably not a good example of the processes of intergovernmental collaboration that are likely to take place under the SUFA. First, the NCB process was heavily conditioned by the intergovernmental context out of which it emerged and which may no longer obtain. Second, the relatively closed nature of the NCB negotiations and its subsequent operation are quite contrary to the principles of openness and citizen engagement enshrined in the SUFA.[54] The program, as it stands, may not necessarily have survived a more transparent and public gestation period.

Negotiations over the NCB took place within a broad context which both demanded and favoured intergovernmental collaboration.[55] In addition, this specific policy area presented circumstances propitious to agreement in that there was "fairly broad agreement among governments … about the priority attached to social policy renewal" without which "efforts at protecting and promoting the idea of the social union would have been dysfunctional, as was

51. Karen Swift and Michael Birmingham, "Caring in a Globalizing Economy: Single Mothers on Assistance," in Durst (ed.), *Canada's National Child Benefit: Phoenix or Fizzle?*, 97.

52. Tom Courchene has referred to this recently as effectively marking a new division of powers between the federal and provincial governments.

53. Swift and Birmingham, "Caring in a Globalizing Economy," 100.

54. See especially, Matthew Mendelsohn and John McLean, "SUFA's Double Vision: Citizen Engagement and Intergovernmental Collaboration," *Policy Options-Options politiques* (April 2000): 44–45.

55. Regarding context, Lazar outlines a range of factors leading the federal government to a more collaborative approach including federal fiscal weakness, increased support for sovereignty in Quebec, demands from the western provinces, decentralist pressures in the Commons in the Bloc Québécois and Reform Party (now the Canadian Alliance), and the ascendancy of the new public management approach in the federal civil service and concomitant growing interest in partnership arrangements. Lazar, "The Federal Role in a New Social Union," 107–8.

the case early in the life of the Chrétien government when it attempted to initiate a national social security review."[56] While the NCB has been characterized as a "natural deal" with no existing contemporary analogues, it could be expected to help contribute to greater likelihood of successful negotiation in more contentious areas in the future. Writing in 1997, Lazar captured this reasoning:

> If ... further substantial progress is made in developing and implementing a more collaborative approach, then a new culture may begin to develop in Ottawa under which federal politicians and public servants become more accustomed to meeting their objectives through a partnership relationship with the provinces. As this approach sinks roots in Ottawa, it will become the new status quo. Later, if and when the influences currently driving Ottawa toward collaboration ease, inertia will work in favour of the new collaboration. [...] If, on the other hand, there is little progress in the next couple of years on the social union front, or if it is confined to only two or three files, then the political and bureaucratic culture is more likely to change at the margins only. The status quo will be unchanged in its foundations.[57]

The actual process of negotiation favoured agreement but partly because it operated quite contrary to the principles espoused in the SUFA. The NCB, announced in the federal budget of 1997, was (not surprisingly) the result of considerable intergovernmental negotiation which was certainly less than transparent.[58] Intergovernmental interactions in this area continue to be marked by the closed nature of intergovernmental relations more generally.[59] Social assistance is not an area that tends to generate sustained public interest. Thus, it is not surprising that the media and public "appeared indifferent to the initiative."[60] Negotiations thus took place in a relatively cool political climate. In contrast to media and public apathy, the reaction of the nongovernmental social-policy community has been characterized as "negative or wary."[61] Large-scale social policies emerging out of protracted federal-provincial negotiations and announced in a federal budget in the face of an indifferent public and resistant social-policy community certainly fit more closely with the existing mode of policy making rather than the new SUFA commitment to effective public participation in developing social priorities.

The closed nature of these negotiations is not out of step with the broader lack of transparency in the field more generally. For example, observers concerned with the effects of the NCB on social assistance rates in the provinces will undoubtedly want to carefully monitor those rates. However, in comparison to the United States, where up-to-date data on average benefits paid are available, the only official Canadian source of comparable data has only recently released figures for 1999. Moreover, the publicly available data on social assistance rates in the provinces are for hypothetical households and the relationship between these rates and actual average amounts paid (data which provincial governments do not make public) is unclear. If Canadian governments are at all serious about developing comparable

---

56. Lazar and McIntosh, "How Canadians Connect," 30.

57. Lazar, "The Federal Role," 109-10.

58. As noted above, it is impossible to determine, for example, the methodology that federal and provincial officials used to arrive at a figure of $1,500 as representative of children's welfare benefits.

59. For example, the provincial reinvestment strategy summary for 1999/2000 (which was initially released in October 1999 and subsequently made publicly unavailable) was not available until just before the time of writing (April 2000). In the words of one official, re-release was delayed pending "federal-provincial politics working themselves out." Knowledgeable officials clearly state that the intergovernmental disagreements blocking the release of this document are not serious. However, this point is crucial in and of itself. In the highly charged atmosphere of intergovernmental relations, even minor intergovernmental disagreements can obliterate opportunities for public transparency. The summary is now available at http://socialunion.gc.ca/NCB-2000/toceng-reinvest2000.html.

60. Battle, "The National Child Benefit," 38.

61. This reaction is not particularly surprising considering that "there are a number of reasons why social policy advocates are particularly leery of governments bearing social policy gifts..." Battle, "The National Child Benefit," 38.

indicators for social programs, comparable average amounts of social assistance actually paid to various categories of recipients is a glaring example of a good place to start.

Rather than highlighting the promise of intergovernmental collaboration, the NCB highlights the problems that may arise when social policy is filtered through collaborative intergovernmental processes. The NCB did not need to be — and indeed was not — sold to the public. The particulars of the agreement (focusing on children's benefits rather than family benefits, emphasizing work incentives for social assistance recipients, and fixing a precise dollar amount at which provinces are absolved of any responsibility for child poverty) appear primarily designed to sell the provinces on the agreement and/or for social service ministers to sell it to their governments. This is not to say that the federal government was pursuing agreement at any cost. However, in the postreferendum political context in which this agreement was reached, officials on all sides must have at least been aware of the high costs of failure. As well, they must have also been aware that slight changes to the definition of the primary policy problem, the NCB's objectives, or the mechanics of the agreement would have risked the agreement running aground on the shoals of intergovernmental politics. To this extent, the agreement appears to embody the requirements of federal-provincial agreement over social policy substance. In this light, the NCB appears to be less about effective social policy trumping a principled respect for the constitutional division of powers. Rather, it is more about what might work in social policy being heavily modified — or even disfigured — by its historical proximity to a battle between one type of federalism (cooperative) and another (a stricter adherence to the division of powers).

It has been fifteen years since Albert Breton penned his reminder of the benefits of competition over collusion and the application of this theory to federal-provincial relations.[62] In contemporary debates, this line of reasoning seems all but forgotten. Some observers argue that collaborative federalism was indeed the model operating in the late 1990s. Others argue that the model in the late 1990s differed considerably from that of the cooperative federalism of the 1960s in which federal-provincial relations were driven by strong trust ties between governments. However, in either case, the general tenor of discussions seems to be one of sympathy for the model whether it is being achieved in practice or not. The familiar refrain is that intergovernmental confrontation is most usually about posturing and not about results. However, this does not mean that confrontation *cannot* be about governments genuinely pursuing results. Social policy is about delivering real services to real people. There are *real* policy differences being debated and the differences between provinces and between the provinces and the federal government are not just about wrangling over jurisdiction. Second, collaboration does not *necessarily* bring good social policy results. Certainly, the example of the NCB suggests that there are good reasons to believe that social policy will suffer when intergovernmental collaboration becomes the primary value in social policy discussions.

Conclusions

Lessons drawn from the example of the NCB for the SUFA are, of course, considerably more suggestive than conclusive. Often touted as an exemplar of the social-union approach, the NCB actually demonstrates the dangers for social policy which may arise in the pursuit of collaborative arrangements. An early assessment of the program suggests that there is no guarantee that collaboration will necessarily produce stronger, more effective social policy than an approach predicated on a greater respect for the existing federal division of powers. If the SUFA compromises federalism values, the NCB suggests that these values may be being sacrificed for the quite uncertain promise of better social policy results.

---

62. See Albert Breton, "The Theory of Competitive Federalism," in Garth Stevenson (ed.), *Federalism in Canada: Selected Readings* (Toronto: McClelland and Stewart, 1989).

Appendix:
Income-tested Benefits in the Provinces

Table 1 compares the proportion of income-tested benefits in each province as a proportion of the implicit social assistance benefits for the first child (or the amount a single parent receives in social assistance minus the benefits he or she would receive as a single employable person). As of 1996, only Quebec offered an income-tested child benefit outside the federal Child Tax Benefit, although this was relatively meager. As of 2000, five provinces offered provincial income-tested benefits — British Columbia, Saskatchewan, Quebec, Nova Scotia and Newfoundland. In these provinces, the increase in income-tested benefits (that is, excluding the $1,020 Child Tax Benefit which existed before these changes) ranges from about one-sixth of the implicit social assistance benefit for the first child in Newfoundland (Newfoundland and Nova Scotia provide only a very meager income-tested benefit) to between 40–60% of the implicit social assistance benefit in Quebec, British Columbia and Saskatchewan. In none of these provinces have these changes resulted in social assistance recipient families receiving less assistance. However, while all three provinces claim to have removed children from the welfare rolls, they have done so by providing an income-tested benefit that is less than half the implicit social assistance benefits they previously provided. Families with children may be less dependent on needs-tested benefits than they were before these programs but by no means is it accurate to state that income-tested benefits available to all low-income persons have replaced social assistance benefits for children. Quebec provides an income-test child-benefit supplement for single parents and this is the sole case where it is even possible to claim that increases in child benefits have been sufficient to "take children off welfare."

Table 1: Income-tested Benefits (Federal and Provincial Combined, 1998) as a Proportion of Implicit Social Assistance Benefits for First Child, 1996**

Province	Implicit First-Child Social Assistance Benefits ($ per annum) 1996**	Single-Parent Family (1 child)SA Income as % of Poverty Line, 1996	Income-tested Benefits ($ per annum) as of July 2000	Increase in Income-tested Benefits ($ per annum) 1996-2000****	Increase as % of Implicit First-Child SA Benefit in Province	Increase as % of Weighted Cdn. Average Implicit First-Child SA Benefit ($5,305)	Increase as % of Lowest Provincial Implicit First-Child SA Benefit (MB=$4097)
Newfoundland	$8760	68%	$2179	$1159	13.2%	21.8%	28.3%
PEI	$4997	64%	$1975*	$955*	19.1%	18.0%	23.3%
Nova Scotia	$4638	64%	$2225	$1205	26.0%	22.7%	29.4%
New Brunswick	$6441	59%	$1975*	$955*	14.8%	18.0%	23.3%
Quebec (Single-Parent Family)	$5280	60%	$4250	$3230	61.2%	60.9%	78.8%
Quebec (Two-Parent Family)***	$5280	51%	$2950	$1930	36.6%	36.4%	47.1%
Ontario	$5349	63%	$1975*	$955*	17.9%	18.0%	23.3%
Manitoba	$4097	52%	$1975*	$955*	23.3%	18.0%	23.3%
Saskatchewan	$4621	63%	$2870	$1850	40.0%	34.9%	45.2%
Alberta	$4464	50%	$1975*	$955*	21.4%	18.0%	23.3%
British Columbia	$5808	63%	$3211	$2191	37.7%	41.3%	53.5%

*No income-tested benefit other than the federal Child Tax Benefit/Canada Child Tax Benefit.

**Implicit first-child social assistance benefits are calculated as the difference between benefits for a single employable person and a single person with one child.

***Implicit first-child benefit for both single parents and dual-parent families is calculated as above based on a single-parent family. However, the difference in this line is the difference between the single-parent income-tested benefit level and income-tested benefits for two-parent families. Single-parent families in Quebec receive an income-tested family allowance supplement of $1,300 per annum.

****Income-tested child benefits as of July 2000 minus existing Child Tax Benefit (1996) of $1,020.

Source: National Council of Welfare, *Welfare Incomes 1996* and various provincial sources for income-tested child benefits, 1998.

CHAPTER FIVE

When Good Times Turn Bad:
The Social Union and Labour Market Policy[1]

Tom McIntosh

Introduction

The last ten years, as the federal government is quick to remind us, has been a period of sustained economic growth characterized by falling unemployment figures, relatively low interest rates and low (almost nonexistent) inflation. Yet at the same time, there remains a palpable sense of unease about the longest period of economic recovery since the end of World War II. Canadians are confronted daily with images that belie the strength of the current economic situation — a perceptible growth in the gap between the rich and poor, the homeless that crowd the streets of the larger urban centres and a sense that the "recovery" of the 1990s is profoundly fragile and that the gains made by some could be easily swept away amidst a coming recession.[2] The early months of 2001 saw a flurry of news reports, many linked to the fluctuations of high-tech stock prices, revised earnings statements from many large corporate actors and drops in consumer spending, that debated whether worries over the use of the "R" word would provoke a self-fulfilling prophecy. Like a proverbial "field of (bad) dreams," if we talked about a recession, it would, some feared, come.

Whatever the reality about the strength and sustainability of the economic growth that Canada has experienced of late, it needs to be recognized just how significant the economic transformation has been in the last decade and a half. The pillars on which the postwar political economy was built have been, for all intents and purposes, removed. Fordism, a strategy of capital accumulation characterized by a high wage, high consumption mode of production resting on the "great compromise" between organized labour, private capital and the state, is no longer a pre-eminent element of North American economic organization. The Keynesian welfare state that reached its pinnacle in the early 1970s has been

---

1. Portions of this chapter appeared as "Is the Social Union Too 'Healthy': Rethinking Labour Market Policy," *Policy Options-Options politiques* (April 2000): 48–49.

2. See, for example: James Laxer, *The Undeclared War: Class Conflict in the Age of Cyber Capitalism* (Toronto: Penguin, 1999); and Mike Burke and John Shields, *The Job-Poor Recovery: Social Cohesion and the Canadian Labour Market* (Toronto: Ryerson Social Reporting Network, Ryerson Polytechnic University, 1999).

reconfigured and restructured into an unrecognizable mutation of what it was.[3] In their place, we have erected different pillars as the basis of the contemporary political economy. First has been the rise of non-Fordist modes of accumulation based on the increased "flexibility" of labour, the increased mobility of capital and a new international division of labour and, second, a pared-back social safety net based increasingly on needs-testing rather than shared citizenship.[4]

None of this is to argue for some return to what has been lost. Both Fordism and Keynesianism belong to an era that has passed and, as critics from both the right and the left would assert, their passing is not entirely lamentable. Rather, what should be of concern is whether the pillars of the current political economy will prove any more resilient than did their predecessors. It may well be the case that the sense of the fragility of the recent recovery stems from the fact that the country has undergone a major shift in direction over these years but the test of that shift has yet to happen. That test will only come when we see whether the social and economic policies that drove the recovery can sustain the nation in the face of recession.

To some extent, it can be argued that Canadians have already made it clear that they are not completely confident that the policy changes of the late 1980s and 1990s are sustainable. Having slain the deficit dragon, having accepted the trade liberalization strategies of the NAFTA and the WTO and having reconfigured much of the social safety net, Canadians appear somewhat subdued at what their governments have wrought. On the one hand, there is pressure on governments to follow their spending cuts with postdeficit reductions in taxation rates. On the other hand, there is growing concern that some elements of the old social union (at least the popular elements) need both a short-term cash infusion and a longer-term "rethinking" in order to preserve and reinvigorate the important role that social policies have played in connecting Canadians. Nowhere is this more true than Canadians' concern with the health of the health system. Survey after survey tells us that Canadians are convinced that the publicly administered health system is "in crisis," but those same surveys indicate an equally high level of satisfaction with the care individuals received within the system.[5]

It is this dichotomy that animates the discussion below. If Canadians are increasingly uneasy with both the sustainability of the recent economic recovery and the current state of the social union, then perhaps the greatest irony in all of this lies in the fact so little attention is being paid to the sector where social and economic policy converge, namely labour market policy. Yet as the political economy of labour markets in Canada have changed in recent years, so too has the governance regime around that policy sector and the policy content of that sector changed. What may be most troubling about these changes is the extent

3. For an extended discussion of these transformations from a Fordist to an increasingly non-Fordist mode of production and their impact on Canadian society and politics, see: Thomas Allan McIntosh, "The Political Economy of Industrial Relations: The State and Concession Bargaining in Canada" (Ph.D. dissertation, Queen's University, 1996), especially chapters 1 and 3; and Tom McIntosh, "Organized Labour in a Federal Society: Solidarity, Coalition Building and Canadian Unions," in Haravey Lazar and Tom McIntosh (eds.), How Canadians Connect (Canada: The State of the Federation, 1998/99) (Kingston: SPS/McGill-Queen's University Press, 1999).

4. For overviews of these transformations, see: Isabella Bakker and Katherine Scott, "From the Postwar to the Post-Liberal Keynesian Welfare State" and Liora Salter and Rick Salter, "Displacing the Welfare State," in Wallace Clement (ed.), Understanding Canada: Building on the New Canadian Political Economy (Kingston: McGill-Queen's University Press, 1997), 286–310 and 311–37; Keith Banting, "The Past Speaks to the Future: Lessons from the Postwar Social Union," in Harvey Lazar (ed.), Non-Constitutional Renewal (Canada: The State of the Federation, 1997) (Kingston: SPS/McGill-Queen's University Press, 1998), 39–70.

5. Senate of Canada, "The Health of Canadians — The Federal Role, Volume One — The Story So Far," Standing Committee on Social Affairs, Science and Technology Interim Report on the State of the Health Care System in Canada (Ottawa: Senate of Canada, 2000), chapter 3.

to which they have been undertaken with little understanding of how such change will reverberate through the lives of Canadians or how changes taken to facilitate increased labour market flexibility in an expanding economy will withstand the challenges of an economic downturn.

The Restructuring of Labour Market Policy

Outside of the context of the negotiations that yielded the so-called Social Union Framework Agreement (SUFA) in February 1999, labour market policy in Canada has itself been significantly restructured over the past decade. If one takes "labour market policy" to mean those measures that relate directly to the supply and demand of labour, then it is possible to characterize two broad categories of policies. First are "passive measures" that provide income support to those temporarily absent from the labour market for any number of reasons and which, in Canada, are characterized by the national Employment Insurance (EI) program and the various provincial social assistance schemes. Second are "active measures" that are designed to facilitate transitions within the labour market, improve labour market skills and promote mobility within the labour market. These are characterized by the myriad of educational, training, and employment measures undertaken by all levels of government in Canada.

There are a number of things that can be said about the current state of labour market policy in this country as it has evolved during the recent period of economic growth. First, the federal EI program (formerly called Unemployment Insurance or UI) has been significantly scaled back. Coverage under the program has fallen precipitously in recent years. The 1995 *Employment Insurance Act* did more than change the name of the program. By changing the terms of benefit receipt from "weeks worked" to "hours worked" and by tightening eligibility requirements for new entrants and re-entrants to the labour market and dropping benefits for "frequent users," the federal government managed to lower coverage of the new program to a smaller percentage of the paid workforce than at any time since the mid-1950s. Both the work of McIntosh and Boychuk[6] and a 1999 study by the Canadian Labour Congress (CLC) that used data from Statistics Canada and Human Resources Development confirm the decline in coverage for the new EI program.[7] For its part, the CLC report concluded that only 36% of the unemployed received benefits in 1998 and that the figure was significantly less in some of Canada's larger urban areas such as Toronto (24%), Ottawa and Regina (19%), Winnipeg (25%), Vancouver (26%), Halifax (29%) and Montreal (33%).[8]

Coincident with, but independent of, the decline in coverage under the EI system has been a similar retrenchment in both the generosity of and eligibility requirements for provincial social assistance schemes. Long considered the refuge of the "deserving poor" and the

---

6. Tom McIntosh and Gerard W. Boychuk, "Dis-Covered: EI, Social Assistance and the Growing Gap in Income Support for Unemployed Canadians," in Tom McIntosh (ed.), *Federalism, Democracy and Labour Market Policy in Canada* (Kingston: SPS/McGill-Queen's University Press, 2000), chapter 3.

7. Both the McIntosh and Boychuk and the CLC studies use calculations of a Benefit-to-Unemployed Ratio (B/U) which takes the number of UI recipients receiving benefits and divides it by the number of unemployed as calculated by the Labour Force Survey. It should be admitted that the B/U ratio is, at best, an imperfect measure of program coverage. Because it relies on the self-identification of unemployment, it tends to under-report the unemployment of seasonal workers who often do not identify themselves as unemployed because, under the Labour Force Survey, they are not "actively seeking employment" — they are simply waiting to go back to their chosen field of work. This results in some instances of the B/U ratio approaching and even surpassing 100%. Still, despite its tendency to inflate coverage in some regions of the country, it provides at least a general outline of the way in which UI/EI provides income support.

8. Canadian Labour Congress, *Left Out in the Cold: The End of UI Coverage for Canadian Workers* (Ottawa: CLC, 1999), passim.

"unemployable," social assistance programs were not intended as a form of income support to the unemployed.[9] Yet it is evident that, as a general feature, social assistance programs are increasingly composed of longer-term recipients with over half of the caseload between 1992 and 1997 being composed of recipients receiving benefits for two or more years.

But, the perception of social assistance rolls being comprised of individuals who are employable may be somewhat misplaced. While long-term recipients may be able-bodied recipients without young children to care for and thus be "employable" in the common-sense understanding of the word, they are also more likely to have fewer and less-relevant job skills by virtue of their distance from the labour market.[10] At the same time, social assistance recipients have also been amongst the most unpopular social policy constituencies. Where UI/EI recipients can claim to have "paid" for their benefits through the premiums deducted from their pay cheques, social assistance recipients are viewed as having to justify their receipt of society's largesse. As a result, these individuals have been subject to a degree of social control and monitoring that is unique within the confines of the welfare state and makes individuals in need less likely to apply for benefits in order to avoid the stigma associated with being a social assistance recipient.[11]

Yet EI may again be the subject of a major overhaul. In response to the perception in Atlantic Canada that residents there have borne the brunt of the 1995 EI reforms, the federal government announced as part of its 2000 election campaign program its intention to reverse the 1995 changes. Given that the governing Liberals were punished at the ballot box by Atlantic Canadian voters in the 1997 election and worried that the newly formed Canadian Alliance Party would make inroads into the Liberal stronghold of Ontario, it became paramount that at least some of the seats lost in Atlantic Canada had to be regained if the Liberals were to win a third majority government. As an electoral strategy, the promise of a return to some version of the old UI system (along with the recruitment of Newfoundland premier Brian Tobin back to federal politics) was enough for the Liberals to regain their dominance in the region. Combined with the Alliance winning only two Ontario seats, the Liberals coasted to a third successive majority with an overall increase in seats that flew in the face of virtually all pre-election predictions.

The remarkable thing about the federal strategy regarding rolling back the 1995 reforms in an effort to regain Atlantic voters is that it rested on a false assumption — namely that Atlantic Canadians have borne the brunt of the decline in EI coverage. While it is true that every region of the country has experienced significant drops in coverage, Atlantic Canada in fact fared better than provinces such as Alberta and Ontario. Because the 1995 reforms retained the differential eligibility criteria for claiming benefits based on regional unemployment rates, those provinces with relatively low unemployment (and especially those with larger proportions of part-time workers) tended to have much sharper declines in coverage. Indeed, the interprovincial variations between provinces was in fact growing in the years immediately preceding and following the introduction of the new EI system.[12]

9. For a fuller examination of the historical and political development of social assistance programs in the provinces and the important variations between them, see: Gerard William Boychuk, *Patchworks of Purpose: The Development of Provincial Social Assistance Regimes in Canada* (Kingston: McGill-Queen's University Press, 1998).

10. McIntosh and Boychuk, "Dis-Covered."

11. For an extended discussion of this element of social assistance policy, see: Margaret Little, *No Car, No Radio, No Liquor Permit: The Moral Regulation of Single Mothers in Ontario, 1920–97* (Toronto: Oxford University Press, 1998).

12. McIntosh and Boychuk, "Dis-Covered," and Tom McIntosh and Gerard W. Boychuk, "Adrift Between the Islands: EI, Social Assistance and the Politics of Income Support for Unemployed Canadians," *Canadian Review of Social Policy* (spring 2001).

What remains to be seen is exactly what form the federal government's new EI system will take. Legislation introduced immediately following the 2000 federal election is aimed directly at increasing benefits and eligibility for Atlantic Canadians and, especially, for those involved in the seasonal fisheries. There is no indication, at this point, that the federal government has any interest in re-examining the impact of the 1995 EI reforms *in toto*. Thus, for those workers in the wealthier parts of the country who continue to struggle with underemployment and labour market instability, there appears to be no relief forthcoming in either the short or medium term. Again, if the Canadian economy moves from its current low levels of growth to a period of contraction, then those workers who are thrown out of the labour market may well find themselves unable to access the benefits of a program for which they have paid. The federal government is missing an important opportunity to take a long, hard look at what the real impacts of the 1995 reforms were and to rethink what role EI has as a form of social insurance.

In the area of active measures, the federal government has effectively devolved its responsibility in this area to most of the provinces over the last number of years. To date all provincial and territorial governments have been given responsibility for active measures except Ontario, though there is some asymmetry in the manner and extent of the devolution that is encompassed by the twelve bilateral agreements.[13] That being said, the general framework consists of the federal government continuing to fund active measures by transferring funds to the provinces, which in turn now design and deliver programs to clients. The rationale for the devolution (though not its impetus, which lay elsewhere) was that the most important labour market for most individuals remained the local one and, as such, the government closest to that market would be best suited to deliver programs tailored to meet the needs of both the local labour market and the individuals within it. Thus, provinces should be the ones to manage and facilitate transitions and movements within those local labour markets. However, the provinces are accountable to the federal government for the effectiveness of the programs delivered under what are called the Labour Market Development Agreements (LMDAs) insofar as the federal government still holds the purse strings.

These changes have had significant impacts. First, individuals and employers are paying premiums for an insurance program (EI) from which an ever-smaller number of unemployed workers are likely to collect. Even recent reductions in premiums have done little to stop the flow of literally billions of dollars into the federal coffers. These contributions were used to balance the federal budget and eliminate its annual deficit.[14] This situation, if it persists, could threaten the political sustainability of the EI program. To some extent, UI's relative acceptance by the Canadian public rested on the sense of "ownership" it provided to the unemployed — they received benefits because they paid premiums. Whatever grumbling about abuses within the system that existed usually occurred at the margins — there may

13. Thomas Klassen, "The Federal-Provincial Labour Market Development Agreements: Brave New Model of Cooperation?," in McIntosh (ed.), *Federalism, Democracy and Labour Market Policy in Canada*, chapter 4.

14. Though often talked about in the popular press, there is no separate "account" into which UI/EI premiums are paid, though in keeping with its origins as an insurance program there was such an account in the past. All premiums paid are deposited into the General Revenue Fund (GRF) and all UI/EI payments are made from that fund. The "EI Account" is, in effect, the difference between the amount collected and the amount paid. Insofar as the program is an insurance fund, it makes sense to keep a reserve fund (to spend less than one collects) to deal with increased demand for benefits in times of economic downturn, but the difference between what is collected and what is spent, even taking into account recent reductions in premiums, is enough to see Canadian workers through a recession the likes of which have never been experienced. Given that there is no "reserve fund" (because there is no separate EI account), the government is then free to use that revenue as a means of balancing its budget. When a recession hits, the increased demand for EI will have to come from the GRF, though the increased demand will be tempered by the decline in eligibility for displaced workers.

have been some resentment about the "dependency" of workers in some regions and numerous anecdotes about those who worked only long enough to get benefits which then financed their winter skiing holidays — but the program remained an important component of the Canadian social safety net.

But insofar as coverage has collapsed and premiums have only declined minimally, it is harder for Canadians to see what exactly is being "insured" and this threatens the political sustainability of the program. As it stands, it is becoming harder for the federal government to justify collecting substantial premiums for a program that offers so little in return.

Provincial governments in wealthier parts of the country, especially Ontario, are also increasingly critical of a program that transfers billions of dollars out of the pockets of provincial workers and employers while transferring so few dollars into the hands of unemployed residents. Similarly, the recent report of the federal auditor general took the federal government to task for misusing EI funds and argued for substantial reductions in premiums so as to bring the cost of the program in line with its coverage. Indeed, the auditor general went so far as to suggest that this misuse of EI funds came perilously close to being in violation of the federal government's constitutional responsibility to run a national unemployment scheme. Yet, it was a previous auditor general who had insisted that the federal government dismantle the separate account for UI monies in the 1980s and insisted that the funds be placed in the GRF. By placing UI monies in the GRF, it became easier for the federal government to effectively "raid" those monies for other purposes. And in the 1990s, Finance Minister Paul Martin used a significant portion of those funds to offset spending cuts and to balance the federal budget. What the current auditor general misunderstands is that the problem with the EI is not that the premiums are too high (and in fact the premiums have been lowered in recent years), but rather that the coverage offered by the program is too low and that it is ceasing to operate as an integral part of the social safety net.

In addition, there is a growing gap in income support for unemployed Canadians as a result of the simultaneous contraction of both EI and social assistance. A growing number of those who find themselves unemployed not only do not qualify for EI, but their situation is such that they do not qualify for social assistance either. The extent and nature of this gap is unclear — the existing data on the interaction between the two pillars of income support provides little in the way of substantive analysis about who the people caught between the programs are or how they sustain themselves while unemployed.[15] Some will have found other work, some will continue to survive on the income of a spouse,[16] some will rely on family and friends for support or will turn to private social agencies. What is clear, though, is that the further stigmatizing of social assistance recipients will result in even fewer of those who do in fact qualify for benefits actually applying for them.

Furthermore, there is no telling whether the LMDAs have yet lived up to their intention of providing better active labour market policies and some serious questions that need to be raised about what will happen to those programs in the event of an economic downturn. As

---

15. McIntosh and Boychuk, "Dis-Covered."

16. The reliance of an unemployed person on his or her spouse's income provides an interesting case study that needs further analysis. It may once have been the case that within married couples where both worked outside the home, one spouse, usually the man, earned significantly more than his wife. Indeed, the stereotypical middle-class picture was one where the wife's employment provided "extra income" to the household. However, the increase in two-professional households, where both partners have significant (if not equal) incomes, has also seen an increase in two-working-poor households where the combined income of both partners may still fall short of a single, middle-class income. Thus, for working-class couples, especially where both work in low-income service-sector jobs, the impact of one spouse's unemployment can be especially devastating — with little in the way of savings or assets to sustain him/herself.

Tom Klassen has argued, the LMDAs have relatively weak accountability measures and a recession will severely test those that exist as demand for increased services on the part of the public is met with provincial demands for increased transfers from the federal government.[17] The provincial governments have few measures in place that can demonstrate the effectiveness of the active measures they are designing and delivering. As such, the federal government may well be loath to increase funding to meet increased demand unless the provinces can conclusively demonstrate that the programs being funded are facilitating transitions within the labour market effectively and efficiently.

Finally, a future recession could well increase intergovernmental conflict over the relative balance between active and passive measures. Labour market policy of late has tended to favour active measures over passive, and changes to each have been consistent with increasing the "flexibility" of workers within the labour market and in making labour policy much more sensitive to the needs of the market.[18] In the event of a recession, unemployment will rise and many of the newly unemployed will neither qualify for EI benefits nor for benefits under more stringent social assistance rules. The federal government will be under pressure to either expand EI eligibility or to increase monies transferred to provinces for social assistance programs. These pressures will be coincident with pressures on both orders of government to increase spending on active labour market measures (e.g. training) and to provide some stimulus to a failing economy. All this will happen at the same time as government revenues begin to fall due to the recession.

What all of this points to is the fact that changes to labour market policy in the last decade and a half have been undertaken by governments with little thought of, first, how changes to specific policies will reverberate through other areas of labour market policy, and, second, how labour market policy may hold up in different economic contexts. Thus, little attention is paid to the interdependencies that exist between specific policies (e.g. the interaction between EI and social assistance) and to overall resiliency of labour market policy in the long term. In short, there has been insufficient attention to the kind of macrolevel analysis of labour market policy that would provide both governments and Canadians in general with the kinds of reassurance needed to allay the anxieties about the sustainability of the recent period of economic growth spoken of above. In the context of the recreation of the Canadian social union, this kind of analysis needs to begin with a discussion about how labour market policy will be governed in the future.

Governing Labour Market Policy in the Social Union

In the minds of the public and, perhaps, in the minds of the political actors involved, the debate about the nature of the Canadian social union has not been focused on labour market policy. For most of those involved, and certainly for the public, the social union is about the health of the health system. The fact that the signing of the SUFA coincided with the transfer of extra dollars to the provinces on the understanding that they would be spent on health care programs only serves to reinforce the primacy of health care, at least for the time being, in the social union debate. The privileged position of the health system was further reinforced in the year and a half following the SUFA's adoption by the signing of the so-called "health accord," which restored federal funding of the health system to the level roughly equivalent to what it was prior to the introduction of the Canada Health and Social Transfer (CHST).

---

17. Thomas Klassen, "Brave New Model."

18. Rod Haddow, "The Political and Institutional Landscape of Labour Market Policy-Making," in McIntosh (ed.), *Federalism, Democracy and Labour Market Policy in Canada*, chapter 2.

Whether the health system's privileged position within the social union debate is justified or not (and it may well be), the risk is that other aspects of the social union could find themselves orphaned within the reform process. Labour market policies occupy a unique position at the nexus of both social and economic policy that makes their overall direction a crucial component of a recreated social union. Yet all too often the field is treated, by the political and bureaucratic executives that shape policy and by the public, as a collection of discreet programs. Little consideration is given to how (and whether) the various parts make up a whole. Thus, political actors call for a national dialogue on the future of Canada's health systems, but no such call is made for strategic thinking around labour market policy in an era of profound economic transformation marked by globalization and increased labour and capital mobility.

While the crisis within the health system is real and demands the attention of both policy analysts and governments, it needs to be emphasized that labour market policy is not unrelated to the health of Canadians. One of the most important determinants of a population's health is secure attachment to the labour market in well-paid, meaningful employment. Parents with (good) jobs tend to be healthier, as do their children. If population health models centred on the "wellness" of individuals is to be a serious element of any renewal of Medicare, then those individuals' relation to the labour market and the policies that have an impact on that relationship need to move closer to the centre of the social policy debate.[19]

As it currently sits, both federal and provincial labour market policies remain almost exclusively focused on only the concerns within a specific program. In short, program changes within the labour market policy field are done, it seems, only in reference to the demands/goals of that specific program and specific political demands around certain issues. The EI reforms of the mid-1990s were undertaken to meet specific federal budgetary goals but without reference to how such changes may or may not have an impact on other areas of labour market policy under either federal or provincial jurisdiction. Neither the EI reforms, the restriction of access to social assistance nor the devolution of active measures was undertaken in reference to any overall conception about the direction of labour market policy in relation to a changing economic order both domestically and internationally.

Yet if reform of labour market policy is to be part of the creation of Canada's social union, then some overall direction needs to be given to the sector as a whole. Rod Haddow has argued that labour market policy has moved increasingly toward making the labour market more flexible and market-friendly in recent years, but it has done so on a relatively ad hoc basis and with little public debate or input.[20] Consequently, business interests have been privileged by the political and bureaucratic elite insofar as corporate interests have access to those policy makers both formally and informally.[21] This only further highlights the greatest

---

19. See, for example: Monica Townson, *Health & Wealth* (Toronto: Lorimer/Canadian Centre for Policy Alternatives, 2000).

20. Haddow, "Landscape."

21. The term "privileged access" is used somewhat advisedly. It should not be taken to mean either that governments listen exclusively to business interests or that business interests speak with a single voice. Indeed, the Chamber of Commerce and the Business Council on National Issues (BCNI) have different perspectives on a wide variety of policy matters. Similarly it should not be taken to imply that governments effectively take their "marching orders" directly from corporate Canada. At the same time, though, the general thrust of labour market policy has been in a more market-friendly direction and "flexibility" and "competitiveness" have been the watchwords. Those are words you will hear more often from the BCNI than from the Canadian Labour Congress. Business interests may not have succeeded in getting all that they want in terms of government policy, but it seems fair to assert that, on balance, organized business interests clearly have the ear of both orders of governments far more often than does organized labour. That some of business' success is really labour's own failings in this regard cannot be ignored either.

irony about the state of labour market policy. Despite consistent and sustained (albeit modest) economic expansion in recent years, the general public's anxiety about their future within the labour market remains unrelieved.

The need for some overarching strategic vision should not be regarded as some call for a Canada Health Act (CHA) for labour market policy — some set of federally enforced guidelines about the nature of what is often provincial policy. Those who call for "national standards" almost always point to the CHA as the prime example of such. But the CHA provides little in terms of real standards — its five core principles are open to significantly different interpretations in different (and even in the same) jurisdictions. Indeed, if the five principles of the CHA were to be given the same meaning in all parts of the country, the health system would soon bankrupt itself ensuring equal access to the same medical services for the residents of Toronto and North Bay.

What is needed with regard to labour market policy is a commitment on the part of governments to take seriously the breadth and scope of labour market policy, its unique position at the nexus of social and economic policy, and to spend significant time understanding how the bits and pieces of policy either do or do not fit together. At the same time, attention needs to be paid not only to how the policy connects with the current economic situation, but how resilient it will be when that situation changes. First and foremost, governments need to commit themselves to coming to grips with the extent of the interaction (both complementary and contradictory) between the various elements of labour market initiatives over which they both have control. Only then can governments begin to think about a "strategic vision" for labour market policy.

The goal of such a strategic vision, however, should not be the articulation of some overarching governance model or single kind of relationship between the federal and provincial governments. The constitutional division of powers slices through labour market policy quite clearly and different forms of intergovernmental governance will likely persist (as they should) relative to different parts of the sector.

What a strategic vision would require is that governments, both individually and collectively, begin to look not only at the trees, but also at the forest. If the intent of the SUFA was to begin a process of clarifying roles and responsibilities while collaborating on the development of common measures and priority setting, then such can only proceed with some level of intergovernmental coordination. Even if the goal is to further disentangle or devolve responsibilities in certain areas (as it was under the LMDAs), such can only proceed within a collaborative framework. Devolution, disentanglement or even centralization will only succeed if it is the outcome of a mutually agreed-upon process. Thus, it might be suggested that the appropriate venue for the development of such a strategic vision is with the Forum of Labour Market Ministers (FLMM). Of course, even the FLMM will not cover all aspects of labour market policy given the manner in which such policy is spread across government ministries, but it would give some kind of institutional support and impetus for the kind of overarching analysis that the sector clearly needs.

But such an undertaking is not without risks for governments. Provinces could well see the FLMM actions in this regard as an attempt by the federal government to insert itself, through the back door, into a policy area where it has only limited jurisdiction. Yet, this need not be the case and is made less likely given the commitments provinces have made to taking an increased role within the sector. The SUFA itself is evidence of a willingness on the part of governments (Quebec excepted) to collaborate on a process of clarifying the roles and responsibilities of each order of government. The goal of such collaboration is not to create mythical, watertight compartments for each order of government, but to recognize:

the sovereignty of both orders of government as well as the growing interdependence between them ... to give rise to a more democratic process ... [that] enables
citizens to be informed about the relative value of different programs. And with the
expanding need for international governance, the requirement for national mechanisms to establish and re-establish a sense of national purpose.[22]

The point is not to involve the FLMM in decision making around specific policy programs
or instruments (e.g. giving the provinces a say in the EI program or the federal government
a role in designing social assistance), but rather to begin mapping labour market policy with
reference to the macrolevel challenges within the Canadian economy and to begin to fill in
the gaps in knowledge about the ways in which the parts interrelate in the creation of the
whole. At best, the FLMM is but a starting point for a rethinking of labour market policy, not
an end point.

By having the FLMM undertake a degree of macrolevel analysis, it becomes possible to
initiate a much more fruitful debate about the direction of specific policy programs by forcing both governments, stakeholders and the public to confront the degree of interrelation-
ships between those program areas. Perhaps most importantly, SUFA provides important
commitments to increase both the transparency and accountability of social policy-making
processes. Thus, the SUFA was not about establishing new modes of intergovernmental
accountability, but rather new kinds of government-to-citizen accountability and transparency. The point was to begin a process where governments report more effectively on the
outcomes of social policy to their citizens and to do so in a manner that would allow citizens
to compare and contrast the actions of both orders of governments. That such reporting
would also allow governments to assess the actions of the other governments is really a by-
product of this intended increase in government-to-citizen accountability.

The increase in government-to-citizen accountability is a component of SUFA's commitment to increasing the engagement of citizens in the deliberations around the future directions for specific programs and policies. Faced with increased public cynicism about the
"behind closed doors" negotiations that characterized intergovernmentalism from the 1970s
through to the mid-1990s (and which culminated with the rejection of the Charlottetown
Accord in a national referendum), governments have, on paper at least, made commitments
to ensure that future non-constitutional renewal of the federation takes place in a more open
environment that involves more active participation by interested publics. Such are noble
sentiments, but in the realm of labour market policy they make necessary the loosening of the
grip of the political and bureaucratic executive and this may well also mean the loss of business' privileged position within the field as a wider array of social and political actors are
allowed on the stage. This, of course, makes the discussion of labour market issues "messier"
as it moves beyond the confines of market-friendly analyses that bureaucratic and business
elites are more comfortable with.

What needs to be emphasized is that any move towards making the FLMM a more robust
body can only be a starting point for a comprehensive approach to the governance of labour
market policy. Having the FLMM undertake a more active role in the mapping of the interdependencies of labour market policies between orders of government would not, in itself,
produce either better policy or better intergovernmental relations in this regard. It might,
however, become the basis on which more successful forms of tripartism or multipartism
could be built and provide opportunities for the legislative branches of both provincial and

---

22. Harvey Lazar and Tom McIntosh, "How Canadians Connect: State, Economy, Citizenship and Society," in Lazar
    and McIntosh (eds.), *How Canadians Connect*, 28.

federal governments to play a more important oversight role in the policy process. This necessarily raises important questions about the nature and extent of the role the FLMM could be expected to play in "planning" or "agenda setting" within the sector.

In the first instance, there is a need to recognize that the FLMM is not (and should not) be directed into collaborative planning towards pan-Canadian national standards or program convergence within the sector. Labour market policy remains multijurisdictional, with both orders of government operating legitimately with regard to different aspects of the sector, and the legitimate role of each order of government needs to be respected. That said, there may be instances where bilateral and multilateral work by governments is appropriate and there needs to be some level of institutional support to undertake that work. Insofar as there exists a need to understand the interdependencies within the sector and that those interdependencies cross jurisdictional lines, then the FLMM may be an appropriate place to begin the analysis of how those different policies interact.

It would also be naïve not to recognize that there exists at the moment little in the way of incentives for governments to undertake even the kind of information sharing that is lacking within the sector. If there is some validity to the notion of the "gap in the middle" with regard to income support, then it has to be recognized that this gap is the result of the successful implementation of specific policy objectives by both orders of government. The point of the EI reforms and the contraction of social assistance eligibility was to reduce the numbers of people on the EI and welfare rolls in order to reduce the costs of the programs to the governments and to reflect the specific ideological outlooks of the governments that implemented the changes. Thus, the off-loading of individuals into a policy vacuum between EI and social assistance is a direct consequence of the successful implementation of the changes to each of the programs.

Analysis that would uncover the nature and the extent of the gap in the middle or would highlight the circumstances of those existing in the middle could in fact begin to generate demands for policy changes in order to reintegrate them into one or the other of the income support programs.[23] As such, it would require governments to recognize that the successful implementation of the reforms in the mid-1990s was, in different terms, in fact a failure. However, the 1997 federal election saw the Liberals virtually shut out of Atlantic Canada, one of their traditional strongholds, which can in part be attributed to the consequences of restructuring of UI into EI.[24] Recently the federal government has lowered premiums moderately, expanded maternity benefits under the program and moved to increase coverage in Atlantic Canada (a move that was rewarded by an increase in Liberal seats in the region following the 2000 federal election). Thus, the government may be beginning to admit that the 1996 reforms were too successful — that is, that the reforms freed up billions of dollars that could be used to balance the federal budget. But whether this translates into a willingness to examine EI's overall role as a means of income support remains to be seen.

Where the FLMM can, it seems, play an effective role without compromising the jurisdictional competence of either order of government is in the realm of outcome measures

---

23. This is most likely, it would seem, to be the case with those who no longer qualify for EI as opposed to those who have been off-loaded from social assistance. To begin with, the recently unemployed have been paying into the EI system directly and therefore may have a politically stronger case than those seeking social assistance benefits who are consistently marginalized within the system.

24. What is ironic in this is that the work by McIntosh and Boychuk cited above demonstrates that in terms of coverage under the new EI, the decline in coverage was disproportionately borne by the wealthier provinces such as Ontario and Alberta. The standard deviation of the B/U ratios shows that the differences between provinces has increased since the 1996 reforms, but that is because the coverage in the wealthier provinces declined at a faster rate than it did in the poorer parts of the country.

and performance indicators. Again, the point would not be to develop some kind of national set of objectives for specific programs, but rather to begin to develop comparable measures between jurisdictions. The specific mix of measures used by any jurisdiction and the relative weight given to particular measures would and should be left to the individual government. The point would be to make the outcomes of labour market policy more transparent to the public, to stakeholders and to governments such that the much-lauded notion of "best practices" becomes more immediately discernible to all concerned. Whether individual provinces choose to alter their policy directions in light of evidence from other provinces is a question best left to the political processes within each province. What is important is that the practices of each of the jurisdictions be readily transparent to the other jurisdictions, not that the policy priorities within the sector be set intergovernmentally. What constitutes "best practices" is a political judgement best made within the political arena, but it is a judgement that can only be made within the context of shared information and a shared understanding of outcomes.

A clearer understanding of the interdependencies within the sector and more transparency around the outcomes of specific policy instruments is the key to a more open policy debate that engages both citizens and stakeholders. The failure of the 1990s experiments with Labour Force Development Boards (LFDBs) should not be taken as meaning that such engagement can not work or should not be encouraged anew. The LFDBs failed for specific reasons in each case[25] and the lack of success with one form of stakeholder engagement does not preclude other experiments in the future. Indeed, such lack of success may demand future experiments designed along different lines. But to some extent, future forays into involving stakeholder groups in a significant manner in the development of policy may in fact rely on a more informed debate that can only occur with better understanding of the interdependencies between labour market programs, better information about outcomes and a robust debate about what exactly constitutes "best practices." Thus, the kind of agenda spoken of above may become the basis on which new experiments with tripartite and multipartite processes are undertaken.

This appears, admittedly, to be a relatively light agenda for the FLMM. But it recognizes both the degree of intergovernmental will necessary to carry out what on the face of it appear to be relatively simple tasks of information sharing and the development of comparable measures and also the need to preserve the relative autonomy of the governments involved. It was noted above that labour market issues are not currently prominent features of the political agendas of either order of government or of the public for that matter. But a future recession will change that, as demand for passive income support increases, the effectiveness of active measures comes under closer scrutiny and the relative balance between active and passive measures becomes more salient. What is evident is the need to begin to move in such a direction before a recession forces governments to respond with policy changes in light of not understanding the interdependencies within the sector or without a better understanding of how particular outcomes are best achieved.

There are of course some important obstacles that will need to be overcome, both institutional and political, for making the FLMM a more robust vehicle for labour market policy debate. First, the FLMM's past work does not provide much in the way of "inspiration" that it is capable of macrolevel strategic thinking around labour market policy. The agendas of the

---

25. The most comprehensive study to date on the LFDB experiments can be found in Andrew Sharpe and Rodney Haddow (eds.), *Social Partnerships for Training: Canada's Experiments with Labour Force Development Boards* (Kingston: SPS/McGill-Queen's University Press, 1997).

FLMM over the past ten years have tended to focus not on high-level issues about the overall direction of labour market policy, but rather on resolving irritants in federal-provincial relations in the field. There appears to be little in the way of institutional memory or resources that would carry debates forward as governments, ministers and officials change. There is evidence in recent years that this is changing, but whether these changes are a trend or a blip is not exactly evident.

Second, insofar as the FLMM includes the government of Quebec, it will need to find a means by which to undertake macrolevel analysis without forcing the Quebec government towards the implementation of an agreement (i.e. SUFA) it explicitly refused to sign. Thus, perhaps, one of the biggest challenges that will need to be met is convincing the government of Quebec that the need for such macrolevel analysis exists independently of any desire to carry forward with the SUFA commitments. This is complicated by the fact that the linguistic divide in the country is mirrored by the existence of separate English- and French-speaking labour markets with relatively minor crossovers between them. If the federal and nine provincial governments are committed to implementing the commitments found within the SUFA, then it may be that there will arise a need for a "two-table" process with a federal government–Quebec table and a federal government-Rest of Canada (ROC) table.

Third, the intergovernmental goodwill that spawned the SUFA (again with the exception of Quebec) may have dissipated somewhat over the past years. In the aftermath of the 2000 election, it appears that western discontent (fueled in part by the Alliance's inability to become a pan-Canadian political party) is on the rise. While the Bloc Québecois suffered a loss of seats in Parliament, the selection of Bernard Landry as Parti Québecois leader and Quebec premier may signal a renewed commitment for that government to hold another referendum on Quebec secession. If that happens, then the controversy over the federal government's so-called "Clarity Bill" (which set out the terms under which Ottawa would accept a vote in favour of provincial secession) could again send a chill over intergovernmental relations. To make matters worse, the move of "the Quebec question" back to the centre of Canadian politics will likely only increase the feelings in western Canada that Ottawa is not listening to its concerns.

Finally, there is a general lack of profile given to labour market policy as spoken of above. Despite persistent anxiety about their status within the labour market and uncertainty about future economic security, Canadians' social policy focus remains on higher-profile issues such as the lack of resources accorded to the health systems across the country. The fact that these personal anxieties do not get expressed in relation to government policy directions makes putting labour market policy on the social union agenda that much more difficult.

In the final analysis, the challenges in moving governments towards a more strategic macrolevel analysis of labour market policy are formidable. Involving the public in that process is an even greater challenge. Whether the FLMM (or some future revamped organization) is an appropriate vehicle, or can be transformed into such a vehicle, is also open to debate. What is clear, however, is that there are a number of choices or possible policy directions that flow out of any attempt to think strategically about the direction of labour market policy. These different choices need to be dealt with in an effort to begin to think more systematically about the future directions of not only specific elements of labour market policy but about the sector more generally.

CHAPTER SIX

Old Wine in New Bottles:
Post-Secondary Education and the Social Union

Herman Bakvis and David M. Cameron

While the term "post-secondary education" (PSE) crops up at least four times in the Social Union Framework Agreement (SUFA), typically in the same breath as health care, social services and social assistance, it is generally conceded that it carries nowhere near the same weight as the highly emotional issue of health care. This relatively lower weighting holds true for both government decision makers and the general public. Further, as we will elaborate below, PSE is only partially covered by the SUFA. For some purposes it can be considered under the heading of social policy, but for others it can be considered part of economic management, for example research and development and labour market programs.

Nonetheless, with or without the SUFA, the PSE sector in Canada is poised to undergo a significant transformation, with certain key provincial governments, such as Ontario's, preparing to put much more into technical and scientific education and much less into the liberal arts. It is a transformation stimulated in part by economic and demographic forces, and in part by government action, with important implications for stakeholders — students, faculty, and citizens. Thus, even if the forces and motives driving these changes are largely economic, the consequences of the changes in the nature of PSE institutions will have social implications for matters such as accessibility. But before turning to these issues and the role that the SUFA may or may not play in these new developments, let us review some evidence on the nature of support for PSE in Canada, paying particular attention to Ottawa's role.

Changing Roles and Responsibilities

Despite the fact that the Constitution Act assigns education to the exclusive jurisdiction of the provinces, save only for certain matters having to do with the protection of religious minorities, PSE has always had a significant federal and intergovernmental dimension. The specific manifestation of federal involvement has changed, to be sure, but its continuing presence and significance cannot be denied, despite Ottawa being less visible and less directly involved in the funding of universities over the past two decades. Indeed, as will be argued in this chapter, we are reaching the point where Ottawa's capacity to influence the overall direction of the PSE sector stands to be considerably enhanced, a development that seems to have at least the tacit consent of the provinces.

Until 1977, federal influence over PSE had gradually and visibly increased in both the university and vocational sectors. The one fly in the ointment was Québec's refusal after

1952 to accept direct federal payments to its universities and colleges, an irritant that was removed in 1959. In 1977, Ottawa appeared to reduce its role in the PSE field when federal transfers to the provinces for PSE were combined with those for health care under the rubric of Established Programs Financing (EPF). The Canada Health and Social Transfer (CHST) of 1995 appeared to reduce Ottawa's role even further, as did its transfer to the provinces of varying degrees of authority over labour market training in the same year. As we will show, however, this appearance is misleading. Over the past decade, Ottawa has been quietly re-asserting its presence in PSE, not through the social policy envelope, but through more targeted measures related to research and economic development.

These changes in Ottawa's role mean that the SUFA may be less relevant to the PSE sector than to other sectors. Ottawa retains, virtually intact, its expansive spending power with respect to direct payments to individuals and organizations, including universities and colleges. Even at the cost of losing Quebec's signature, Ottawa refused to budge on this, except for a modest commitment to "give at least three months' notice and offer to consult." Current federal initiatives in research, and its longstanding involvement in student aid, will presumably proceed unimpeded by the SUFA.

Meanwhile, PSE has all but disappeared from public attention in discussions of the CHST and the partial restoration of federal transfers. The provinces certainly treated the increased funds forthcoming with the SUFA, and further increases in the federal budget of October 2000, as though they were earmarked for health. Led by Ontario, the provinces seem also to be shifting their priorities in PSE in favour of technical and vocational programs, and in ways that enhance the capacity of their universities to maximize their share of federal research grants. In both areas, we may well be witnessing the forging of a new federal-provincial division of labour in PSE, outside of the SUFA.

What seems to be happening is that Ottawa has finally accepted the error of its ways in trying to create a constitutional distinction and jurisdictional division between education and training. That distinction never had much reality on the ground anyway, which mostly took place in provincial colleges. But accepting a more inclusive notion of education has not meant the triumph of academic over vocational values in PSE. Provincial governments are just as capable as Ottawa of appreciating the potential for education to be used as an instrument of economic growth. This is paving the way for a new intergovernmental accommodation in PSE, but it is an accommodation based on economic priorities and may therefore have little to do with the SUFA.

Early Federal Initiatives

The earliest manifestations of federal involvement came as the result of jurisdiction in areas that overlapped with education, or were the legacy of previous constitutional arrangements.[1] Thus, for example, when the Royal Military College (RMC) was established in 1874 under federal legislation, it was justified as being a matter primarily concerning defence, even though it also served to train civilian engineers. And when it finally obtained the power to grant university degrees in 1959, it did so under legislation enacted by Ontario. The RMC was not the only college to run into this kind of jurisdictional crossfire. Its next-door neighbour, Queen's, ended up with both federal and provincial charters in 1882, after a Privy Council decision on another matter put its 1874 provincial act in doubt. There were also a few cases of colleges incorporated under private federal legislation, but these either came to naught or were subsequently transformed into provincial institutions.

---

1. See David M. Cameron, *More than an Academic Question: Universities, Government, and Public Policy in Canada* (Halifax: IRPP, 1991).

The real impetus for a federal role in PSE came early in the twentieth century with the emergence of an industrial economy. By 1901, the Dominion Trades and Labour Council and some of the larger boards of trade were actively pressuring the federal government to get involved. By 1910, they had succeeded in persuading the federal government to establish the Royal Commission on Industrial Training and Technical Education. Perhaps one of the most telling features of this commission, especially given the posture later taken by some provinces, was that it was established only after all provincial governments, including Quebec, had agreed. The general consensus at the time was that vocational and technical education could be considered a federal responsibility specifically under the trade and commerce power, as well as the more general federal concern for economic management.

Even before the royal commission reported, the federal government made a further move in this respect, enacting legislation in 1912 and 1913 to provide for its first-ever conditional grant program, covering instruction in agriculture, with a fund of $10 million. The royal commission reported during the latter year, but its recommendations were shelved until the end of World War I. Then, in 1919, the federal Technical Education Act set aside another $10 million for this purpose, on a cost-shared basis with the provinces. Only Ontario managed to use up its quota of federal funds within the ten years originally prescribed, and the provision had to be extended no fewer than four times before it was finally completely taken up by 1948. Conditional grants, priority-shifting though they may be, obviously do not always induce the intended provincial behaviour.

Meanwhile, a second dimension of federal involvement in PSE had also emerged from the growth of industry and the pressures of war. This was university-based research, which was given force and direction with the establishment of the National Research Council (NRC) in 1916. And because the only significant research capacity that existed, or could reasonably be cultivated, was located within universities, the NRC was ineluctably drawn into a close working relationship with universities and with individual scholars, through scholarships and research grants.

Postwar Boom and Post-Secondary Education

The postwar revolution in PSE began with the waves of returning veterans that flooded university campuses, beginning before the war was over and reaching its peak at 35,000 in 1946–47. This was on top of a civilian enrolment of just over 45,000 in the same year. The veterans came with federal allowances, and the universities that accepted them also received federal grants. And when those allowances began to peter out, the universities set to work lobbying for the continuation of federal support. They found a receptive sponsor in the Massey Commission, the Royal Commission on National Development in the Arts, Letters and Sciences. The commission, comprised almost entirely of people closely associated with universities, duly recommended the introduction of federal grants to universities in its 1951 report.[2] The government, under Prime Minister Louis St. Laurent, accepted the recommendation and money began flowing within the year. The manner of its distribution was interesting in at least two respects.

First of all, the money, which amounted to $7.1 million per year, was divided among the provinces on the basis of 50¢ per capita. Then, each provincial allotment was divided among the eligible institutions on the basis of enrolment. This meant, of course, that institutions received no recognition for out-of-province students or above average participation rates, with the result that a province like Nova Scotia received much smaller grants per student

---

2. In 1940 the Rowell-Sirois report had also raised the possibility of federal grants to universities, but perceiving a possible conflict of interest had refrained from actually recommending them.

than some other provinces.[3] Second, the grants were paid without regard for religious affiliation; the only criterion was that work be recognized as being beyond junior matriculation. This, of course, was a godsend for many of the small, denominational colleges, such as those in the Maritimes, and no doubt helped shape the future of PSE policy in several provinces. At the same time, it violated the policy of some other provinces, like Ontario, which had historically refused public support for denominational institutions.

All of the provinces accepted the federal grants for 1951–52, but opposition soon mounted in Quebec, and the grants were refused thereafter. The stalemate continued until a change of government occurred in Ottawa in 1957 and the death of Quebec premier Maurice Duplessis in 1959. A new deal was struck between Ottawa and Quebec that was to have major long-term consequences for fiscal federalism in Canada. The grants to universities were scrapped in Quebec, in favour of a fiscal transfer. The amount of money was the same, but the method of payment was profoundly different. Quebec received the revenue derived from a one-percentage, point corporate income tax abatement, adjusted to yield revenue equal to the foregone grants. Meanwhile, the value of those grants was periodically increased, to $1 per capita in 1956, $1.50 in 1958, $2 in 1963, and finally to $5 in 1966. That year ushered in a radical change in federal-provincial relations with respect to all of PSE.

Meanwhile, direct grants to universities were by no means the only form of federal support. The Canada Council was established in 1957 with a $50 million endowment from which it was authorized to provide grants for university research in the arts, humanities and social sciences. The endowment was subsequently increased to $100 million in 1961, and to $150 million in 1964. The Canada Student Loans Program (CSLP) was introduced in 1964, replacing a modest earlier scheme that had been in existence since 1939. Interestingly, this time the program provided for provinces to opt out and receive comparable levels of federal support. Then, following the release of the Hall Royal Commission on Health Care in 1964 and in support of the decision to proceed with a national shared-cost program for health-care insurance, the federal government introduced the Health Resources Fund in 1966, worth $500 million over fifteen years in grants for expanded health facilities, mostly in universities. And then, as if to top things off, the federal government arranged for the secondment of Robin Ross, registrar of the University of Toronto, to advise on the creation of an education support branch in the Department of the Secretary of State. It looked for all the world like the federal government intended to claim a more formal and explicit role in respect of PSE. Indeed, the provinces were sufficiently alarmed at this prospect that they banded together to create the Council of Ministers of Education, Canada (CMEC). It began its operations with a decidedly anti-Ottawa bias, even refusing federal requests to attend its meetings.

As it turned out, changes were in store that pointed in a very different, but equally dramatic, direction. These changes had to do with vocational training, and in particular with a new concept that captured the federal imagination: manpower, or adult occupational training.

A New Federal Policy: Manpower Training

In the fall of 1966, Prime Minister Lester Pearson outlined the direction of a dramatic turn in the course of Canadian federalism, including a new federal initiative with respect to PSE. It came in two parts, one marking a federal policy retreat and the other a bold new initiative.

In retreat, the federal government decided to abandon its direct involvement in financing universities. It would keep its hand in research and student loans, save for any province which opted out of the latter (with compensation), but it would no longer make grants to

---

3. In 1951–52 the per capita value of the grants varied from a low of $92 in Nova Scotia to a high of $483 in Newfoundland.

universities. Instead, it would transfer money to the provinces, partly in a one-time transfer of tax points and the balance annually in cash, through its new Fiscal Arrangements Act.

In stark contrast to this accommodation with the provinces, the federal government set forth a new and comprehensive claim to the occupational training of adults under the Adult Occupational Training Act (AOTA). On constitutional grounds, the prime minister held that this was not education at all but training, for economic purposes, of adults already out of school and in the labour force. The ensuing clash of grand designs, between federal economists and provincial educationists, especially as it played out in Ontario, has been chronicled else-where.[4] Suffice it to say here that the provinces did not accept the distinction between education and training, which was artificial in any case, although some of them were more sympathetic than others to the use of training for economic purposes. Virtually all of the provinces opposed the federal training agenda and conspired to insist on an exclusive brokerage role for themselves, coming close to re-establishing a *de facto* shared-cost relationship.

The federal plan was certainly comprehensive. In its most ambitious articulation, it proposed to be nothing short of an integrated approach to all aspects of the occupational training of adults, including recruitment, counseling, placement and the payment of training allowances to individuals selected by federal officials in response to training needs identified by federal analysts. The one element in the package that federal officials did not propose to provide themselves was the actual training. This they intended to purchase from provincial agencies or from private providers. At the centre of the ensuing controversy was this attempt by federal officials to treat provincial colleges and other institutions as competitive purveyors of training, from whom federal officials might purchase "seats" on behalf of their clients. Indeed, the federal proposal envisaged shifting its purchases to the private sector if the price and product were preferable.

In fact, neither element in the federal strategy turned out as intended. On the university side, the scheme which had been designed to work mostly through the tax side, quickly assumed all the characteristics of a shared-cost program, and an expensive one at that. On the training front, it became evident that federal analysts were not able to identify training needs with anything like the degree of precision they had anticipated. Moreover, provincial officials were successful in frustrating federal designs. Some provinces, especially Ontario, Québec, Alberta and British Columbia, successfully parlayed federal training dollars into institutional support for their emerging binary PSE systems, in which colleges came to comprise the more vocationally oriented complement to universities.[5] While some of the other provinces were slower and less aggressive in steering federal resources to the general support of their college systems, they all eventually came to adopt similar policy orientations.

By the early 1970s Canada was experiencing the new phenomenon of "stagflation," inflation and economic stagnation occurring simultaneously. Then the economic roof fell in with the OPEC oil crisis. The upshot was a sea change in federal-provincial relations, which was given particular force and direction by the political priorities of Prime Minister Pierre Trudeau. For PSE, and especially universities, the postwar boom that had continued through the 1960s came to a crashing end. The signs were everywhere and obvious, and governments began to respond accordingly. Predictions of large numbers of unemployed graduates were

---

4. J. Stefan Dupré et al., *Federalism and Policy Development: The Case of Adult Occupational Training in Ontario* (Toronto: University of Toronto Press, 1973).

5. The provinces differed considerably in their development of college systems. Québec created a kind of binary divide within its *collèges d'enseignement général et professionnel* (CEGEPs), as did Alberta and British Columbia with their university-level as well as occupational and professional programs. Ontario kept its colleges and universities quite distinct except under specific arrangements with specific institutions. The other provinces were generally slower in developing mature college systems and kept closer to what the federal government was willing to pay for.

common. In 1971 enrolment fell well below university expectations and in 1972 it actually declined in absolute terms. Signalling things to come, the federal government that year capped annual increases in its grants to the provinces for PSE.

Beginning in 1977, a new fiscal arrangement was put in place, with Established Programs Financing (EPF) covering both health and universities. In the same year, the federal government reorganized its support for university research, creating three new granting councils out of the National Research Council and the Canada Council, respectively for health, science and engineering, and the social sciences and humanities. But it did not increase its funding accordingly.

The final Trudeau mandate was preoccupied with two priorities so far as PSE was concerned. On the one hand, there was a series of attempts, progressively more draconian in nature, intended to curtail federal spending and with it the seemingly uncontrolled deficit. PSE in particular, and federal-provincial transfers in general, provided ready targets for these measures. On the other hand, the federal government was growing increasingly frustrated with the outcomes of its PSE spending and particularly its seeming inability to achieve its policy objectives in either the university or adult training sectors.

The EPF arrangement had been premised on the development of a new, cooperative spirit in federal-provincial relations, at least respecting university finance. Instead, the provinces rebuffed federal overtures at every turn. To make matters worse, it was apparent that provincial spending was being reduced as federal transfers increased.[6] Yet the federal government did not seem to be getting political credit for its efforts. Almost before the ink was dry on the new arrangement, the federal minister of Finance, Alan MacEachen, warned that the federal government wanted to reopen negotiations in order "to achieve significant savings."[7] The provinces seemingly paid no attention, partly no doubt because the arrangement could not be altered without several years' notice. The federal government was equally dissatisfied with developments on the manpower training side. It had not been able to gain control over training priorities and remained seemingly locked into funding provincial programs. In response it launched a number of studies in both areas of PSE.[8]

The study that captured considerable attention was the report on labour market training by the then Queen's University economist, David Dodge. He argued that federal spending on universities was already more than adequate and weighted too heavily in favour of general arts, and that the priority for the future should be shifted to the training of workers already in the labour force. Obviously impressed with Dodge's argument, the federal government responded in 1982 by replacing the AOTA with new legislation, the National Training Act (NTA). It was designed to shift federal purchases away from provincial colleges and towards private industry, and away from basic upgrading and in favour of higher-level skills training, but it achieved only limited success during what remained of the Trudeau mandate.

6. Peter Leslie noted that 7 of the 10 provinces reduced their own expenditures between 1978 and 1980, substituting federal transfers. See Peter M. Leslie, *Canadian Universities, 1980 and Beyond: Enrolment, Structural Change and Finance* (Ottawa: AUCC, 1980), 379.

7. Cited in Cameron, *More than an Academic Question*, 236.

8. Canada, Parliamentary Task Force on Federal-Provincial Fiscal Arrangements, *Fiscal Federalism in Canada* (Ottawa: Minister of Supply and Services, 1981) (Breau task force); Employment and Immigration Canada, Task Force on Labour Market Development, *Labour Market Development in the 1980s* (Ottawa: Minister of Supply and Services, 1981) (Dodge report); Parliamentary Task Force on Employment Opportunities for the 1980s, *Work for Tomorrow: Employment Opportunities for the 80s* (Ottawa: House of Commons, n.d.).

If at First You Don't Succeed...

Real change in federal policy had to await a change of government and the election of the Mulroney Progressive Conservatives in 1984. They moved quickly, and in 1985 launched the Canadian Jobs Strategy (CJS). The CJS continued to exhibit many of the structural weaknesses and contradictions that had come to characterize federal policy in labour market training, but in one respect it represented a sharp break with the past. This time, the federal government did succeed in shifting federal spending away from provincial colleges and into the private sector, and it did this while reducing total spending on training. The result was that provincial colleges received smaller slices of a shrinking pie.[9] Needless to say, the provinces were not particularly happy with this development, and labour market training continued as a noticeable irritant in federal-provincial relations.

A second shift in federal training policy under the Mulroney government came in 1989 as the result of the Canada-U.S. free trade agreement. This time, federal policy took a decided turn, embracing through its Labour Force Development Strategy (LFDS) the institutional underpinnings of European-style corporatism with its reliance on training policy dominated by direct business and labour participation. A hierarchy of labour force development boards was envisaged, at local, provincial and national levels, but the provinces were not about to accept a subordinate role in this area, and either created their own provincial bodies or allowed those created by federal initiative to atrophy.[10] Moreover, the federal government was still driven by its overarching commitment to deficit reduction and drew increasingly upon the unemployment insurance fund to finance its training expenditures. This, in turn, further narrowed the reach of federal training dollars, since only unemployed UI clients had access to these dollars. Provincial attitudes, cool at best for some time, turned increasingly frosty. Federal policy had succeeded in frustrating provincial ambitions on the PSE training front, but it had failed to establish a viable alternative, either by the federal government itself or in conjunction with business and labour partners.

The Mulroney government's penchant for private sector participation was evident also on the research front. In 1986 it introduced a program of matching funds by which future increases in funding for the federal research councils would be tied to private sector contributions. In the event, the definition of private sector was so broad that the maximum expenditure of $380 million over four years was quickly and easily reached. The Senate committee on national finance found the program to be seriously flawed, offering no evidence that it had actually induced any increase in private-sector spending.[11] A much more successful program followed in 1988. It grew out of the National Advisory Board on Science and Technology, a body composed of senior government, university, and private-sector officials and chaired by the prime minister. It was modeled on a similar initiative by the Peterson government in Ontario, and involved the establishment of a series of "networks of centres of excellence." This was a new idea in Canada, bringing together researchers from a variety of universities and private laboratories into a network or "virtual" centre, focusing on a specific theme or project. Perhaps what was most significant about this initiative was the fact that it marked

---

9. For an excellent review of this period, see Rodney Haddow, "Federalism and Training Policy in Canada: Institutional Barriers to Economic Adjustment," in François Rocher and Miriam Smith (eds.), *New Trends in Canadian Federalism* (Peterborough: Broadview Press, 1995), 338–68.

10. Andrew Sharpe and Rodney Haddow, *Social Partnerships for Training: Canada's Experiment with Labour Force Development Boards* (Ottawa and Kingston: Caledon Institute and School of Policy Studies, Queen's University, 1997).

11. Senate, Standing Committee on National Finance, *Twenty-Sixth Report*, 47:16 (July 27, 1988).

the first substantial increase in federal spending on research in some years. A total of $1.3 billion in additional money was pledged over the next five years, $240 million of it for the networks and $200 million for regular research grants through the three granting councils.

An interesting phenomenon was beginning to emerge on the research front. Without any formal agreement to this effect, a kind of *de facto* division of labour was emerging between federal and provincial governments. In different ways, a number of the provinces were discovering that they could lever federal research support for their province's universities. Quebec was perhaps the first to do this in a systematic and effective manner, through its *Fonds pour la formation des chercheurs et l'aide à la recherche* (Fonds FCAR) established in 1981, but Ontario, Alberta, and British Columbia were also increasingly active in supporting the development of infrastructure and designated research centres that could then compete with advantage for federal research funds. Nova Scotia adopted a similar strategy in its new funding formula introduced in 1998.[12]

Meanwhile, transfers to the provinces for PSE were being squeezed. By 1985 the federal government had seemingly given up on trying to re-establish any provincial obligation to use federal transfers under EPF for their designated purposes. Then it began a process that seemed destined to program federal transfers for PSE to wither away. First, it dropped the EPF "escalator" (the rate at which provincial entitlements automatically increased) from the gross national product (GNP) to GNP-2%. Then, in 1989 it reduced it further to GNP-3%, and a year later it suspended the escalator altogether. The focus of federal priorities seemed increasingly to be centred on research and training, and less on general support of universities and colleges. But it had still not found an effective accommodation with the provinces in managing the training function.

Then came the bombshell of the Charlottetown Accord, and its proposal to recognize provincial jurisdiction over training, throwing in the federal towel in an intergovernmental dispute that had lasted a quarter of a century. The accord, agreed to in 1992, would have added labour market development and training to Section 92 of the Constitution Act, confirming this as an area of exclusive provincial jurisdiction and requiring the federal government to withdraw from existing programs at provincial request. Conversely, the federal government would be obliged to continue its involvement if a province so requested. The accord also brought to the surface the longstanding federal interest in formally recognizing a constitutional commitment of both orders of government to the preservation and development of Canada's "social and economic union." The Charlottetown Accord died, of course, at the hands of a national referendum, but both of these proposals would live to see another day. Not, however, before one more attempt was made to redefine a federal role in PSE and training.

The Conservatives, by then under Prime Minister Kim Campbell, had undertaken a major reorganization and consolidation of cabinet portfolios, the main features of which were continued under the new Liberal government of Jean Chrétien, elected in October 1993. Chrétien appointed Lloyd Axworthy to the Human Resources Development portfolio and gave him a mandate to develop policy proposals covering unemployment insurance, social assistance, job training and PSE. His discussion paper, released a year later, proposed a radical change in the federal government's approach to supporting PSE.[13] It would scrap the PSE component of EPF, and with it transfers to the provinces, and substitute a system of loans directly

---

12. David M. Cameron, "Equity and Purpose in Financing Universities: The Case of Nova Scotia," *Canadian Public Administration* 43, no. 3 (2000): 296–320.

13. Canada, *Agenda: Jobs and Growth, Improving Social Security in Canada* (Ottawa: Minister of Supply and Services, 1994).

to students, based on the income contingent repayment principle. It was a clever design, to be sure, but it was fatally flawed, not least because of its differential impacts on the provinces.[14] In the event, the Liberals killed the plan themselves when the 1995 budget prescribed unprecedented cuts in program spending. EPF was not abolished. Rather, it was dissolved, along with the Canada Assistance Plan (CAP), into the new Canada Health and Social Transfer (CHST). The cash portion of the new CHST would be cut from $18.5 billion under CAP/EPF in 1995–96 to $12.5 billion by 1998–99.

Noteworthy is the fact that while the CHST refers to "health" and "social" spending, in its title there is no explicit reference to PSE. And while under the Canada Health Act there are specific provisions that constrain provinces from allowing practices like extra billing by physicians, there is no comparable legislation covering PSE. Practices, such as differential tuition fees imposed on out-of-province students by the province of Quebec, and Quebec's refusal to allow its student loan program to be used for out-of-province studies, appear potentially to be violations, if only in spirit, of one or more of the five principles governing the CHST. While these practices have only limited effects, and Quebec's out-of-province fees, for example, are set at the national average, other provinces such as British Columbia have also toyed with the idea of imposing differential fees. With the rise in tuition fees, discrepancies between provinces are growing, and in the long run these developments may increase unfairness and limit mobility. There is some argument, therefore, that governments should begin thinking about whether certain rules should be put into place, or existing rules revised, in order to give more concrete meaning to the five basic principles, particularly concerning accessibility, universality and mobility. If such discussions were to take place, the governments in question might consider moving closer to the health-care model, where, for example, the costs of treating out-of-province patients are billed to the patients' home province. Thus, in a comparable example under PSE, the true costs of educating an out-of-province student (i.e. costs beyond those covered by tuition fees) would be borne by his/her home province. Such measures, of course, are bound to be controversial, since some provinces, Nova Scotia for example, where a very high proportion of PSE students are out-of-province, would stand to benefit, while others, Quebec for instance, would likely suffer a net outflow. Nonetheless, one could argue that if the SUFA is going to have any meaning, some discussion of what its principles mean in practice for PSE is desirable.

The other area that warrants discussion between Ottawa and the provinces is student assistance. Beyond tuition fees, financial assistance to students is the issue of most direct concern to students and their families. When Ottawa cut PSE funding under the CHST, it did maintain its commitment to the venerable Canada Student Loan Program, operated in partnership with most of the provinces.[15] Indeed, in 1994 it expanded the program, raising the weekly loan limit of $105 per week (which had remained frozen since 1984) to $165 per week and introduced a program of "Special Opportunities Grants," designed for students with disabilities and part-time students and women in certain disciplines. In 1998 students with dependants also became eligible for these grants, renamed "Canada Study Grants." At the same time, in 1995 Ottawa stopped guaranteeing Canada Student Loans and instead began paying a risk premium to financial institutions for providing the loans. Furthermore, changes

---

14. See David M. Cameron, "Shifting the Burden: Liberal Policy for Post-Secondary Education," in Susan D. Phillips (ed.), *How Ottawa Spends 1995–96: Mid-Life Crisis* (Ottawa: Carleton University Press, 1995), 177.

15. Essentially the provinces administer the federal program in conjunction with their own, in effect allowing for a common application procedure for students. Quebec and the Northwest Territories operate their own programs and receive alternative payments from Ottawa.

in the Bankruptcy and Insolvency Act excepted student loans so that persons declaring bankruptcy are not allowed to discharge debts in the form of student loans. While intended to deal
with deadbeat students, it has resulted in considerable hardship for more legitimate cases.
These changes resulted in a certain amount of controversy, when later some financial institutions withdrew when the premium proved insufficient to cover losses on student loan
defaults. In the eyes of some, the system has serious deficiencies that need to be addressed.[16]
The preservation and, indeed, enhancement of the federal student loan program, however,
was overshadowed by other changes that affected the PSE sector, changes that stemmed in
good part from cuts in transfer payments to the provinces.

The year 1995 produced more than a massive reduction in federal-provincial transfer payments for PSE along with other programs. It also witnessed a referendum in Quebec which
very nearly yielded a mandate to separate. In campaigning for the "no" side, Prime Minister
Chrétien promised to turn over to the provinces full control of labour market training. This
offer was expanded in 1996 to include additional labour market tools, such as counseling and
other active measures administered by the National Employment Service. Subsequently,
Ottawa reached agreement with most provinces that saw seven of the provinces and territories taking over primary responsibility for labour market development with the remaining
provinces and territories, excepting Ontario, reaching so-called co-management agreements
with Ottawa.[17] These agreements, negotiated and signed in 1997, are set to expire soon, and
it appears that provinces with co-management agreements (where Ottawa and the province
jointly deliver programs) will request that they too move to devolution type. Ontario is the
sole province that does not yet have an agreement. It appeared, therefore, that by 1995
Ottawa had essentially conceded defeat on both fronts, that is, withdrawing not only from
the PSE sector, as it had done in the 1960s, but also from labour market training, the area it
originally staked out as an important economic development tool when it ceased having a
direct role in PSE.[18]

The apparent retreat by Ottawa from PSE within the framework of the CHST has been
seized upon by the provinces. According to a report prepared last year by the British
Columbia government, federal spending on transfers to the provinces for PSE has declined
from 3.3% of its total budget in 1979–80 to 1.6% in 1998–99.[19] The results, claims the report,
"have fundamentally affected the underpinnings of post-secondary institutions across
Canada." And further

> the cuts have also caused fragmentation of the Canadian system of post-secondary
> education as a result of the pressures put on the provinces by the federal reductions.
> This fragmentation is manifested especially in growing differences in tuition fees,
> debt loads and enrollment rates for students across the country.[20]

---

16. Madelaine Drohan, "Students need a loan program that works," *Globe and Mail* (December 9, 2000).

17. Herman Bakvis, "Checkerboard Federalism? Labour Market Development Policy in Canada," in H. Bakvis and
    G. Skogstad (eds.), *Canadian Federalism: Performance, Effectiveness and Legitimacy* (Don Mills, ON: Oxford
    University Press, 2002); Herman Bakvis and Peter Aucoin, *Negotiating Labour Market Development Agreements*
    (Ottawa: Canadian Centre for Management Development, 2000).

18. See Rodney Haddow, "The Political and Institutional Landscape of Canadian Labour Market Policy-Making," in
    T. McIntosh (ed.), *Federalism, Democracy and Labour Market Policy in Canada* (Kingston: Institute of
    Intergovernmental Relations, 2000).

19. British Columbia, *Federal Spending on Post-Secondary Education, Transfers to Provinces: Trends and Consequences*
    (Victoria: Ministry of Advanced Education, Training and Technology, 1999).

20. Ibid.

Figure 1. Provincial governments spent a smaller proportion of their budgets on education in the 1990s.

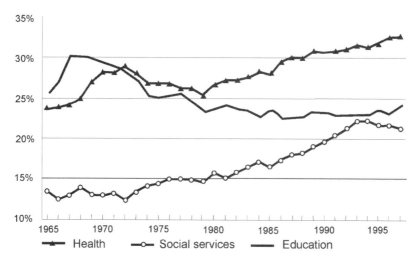

Source: AUCC, Trends (*Ottawa: n.p.,* 1999), 2.

It is this decline in support from Ottawa, according to the provinces, which in large part explains why the provinces have been spending less on PSE. As can be seen in Figures 1 and 2, provinces have been spending less on education generally and on PSE in particular. In Figure 1 it is obvious that education spending is being crowded out primarily by health-care spending; and within the category of education spending, as shown in Figure 2, PSE is being squeezed by spending on primary and secondary schooling. Most of the shortfall in the decline in transfers to PSE institutions has been made up by tuition fee increases. As can be seen in Table 1, while government transfers have declined by 25%, revenues from tuition fees have increased by 67% since 1992. It is clear that governments and universities have placed the burden of making up lost revenues resulting from government cuts on the students and their families.

For students and their parents there is no clear relief in sight. In the February 2000 federal budget, Finance Minister Paul Martin committed an extra "one-time" payment of $2.5 billion under the CHST, an amount the provinces regard as negligible.[21] Provincial premiers say it will have minimal impact in reducing their health-care costs. None has mentioned that any of the $2.5 billion will flow to the PSE sector. On the face of it, the argument seems clear that governments at both levels should be doing more to restore lost funding to ensure that PSE institutions remain accessible to all qualified students. Yet it may not be that simple. Despite the cuts in recent years, Canada remains near the top of the league among OECD nations when it comes to support for PSE and for education generally. Thus, according to 1995 OECD data, Canada spent from both public and private sources (in U.S. dollars) $11,471 per PSE student compared to the OECD average of $8,134 and second only to the U.S. with $16,262.[22] When these figures are expressed as a proportion of GDP, Canada actually comes out on top. As can be seen in Figure 3, spending in Canada on PSE represented 2.5% of GDP versus 2.4% in the U.S. and well above the OECD average of 1.3%. When one takes into account that in Canada a much larger proportion of PSE spending comes from government

21. "Provinces given $2.5-billion infusion," *Globe and Mail,* February 29, 2000.

22. *Education Indicators in Canada: Report of the Pan-Canadian Education Indicators Program 1999* (Ottawa: Statistics Canada/Council of Ministers of Education, Canada, 2000), 58.

Figure 2.

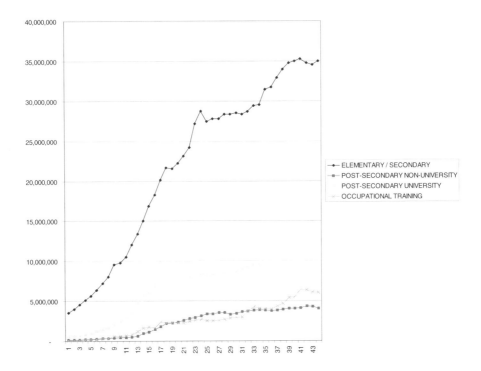

Figure 3. Education indicators in Canada: Report of the Pan-Canadian Education Indicators Program 1999

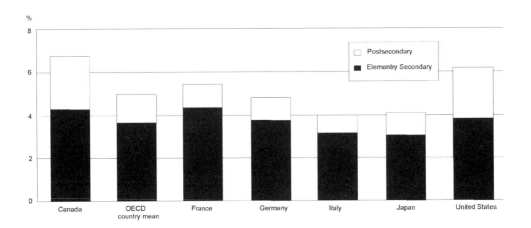

Source: Ottawa: Statistics Canada/Council of Ministers of Education, Canada, 2000, p. 58.

Table 1
Universities — Funding Sources

	Operating income ($1,000)	Constant $1992 per student	Rate of change since 1992
Government	4,831,835	6,807	-24.0%
Fees	2,410,248	3,395	67.0%
Gifts and donations	71,225	100	29.0%
Other	309,209	436	45.0%
Total	7,622,517	10,738	-6.0%

Source: AUCC, *Trends*.

sources compared to the U.S., this means that Canadian governments also probably spend more in absolute dollars relative to all other countries.

Of course, one can argue that 2.5% of GDP is still not enough to provide a high-quality education to all those who qualify for entry to a PSE institution. But here the question arises, certainly in the minds of government decision makers, of whether Canada can afford a high-quality PSE system with access guaranteed to anyone with a high-school diploma. Given that enrollments have risen considerably and will continue to rise not only with population growth but also with an increase in the participation rate of those of university age, such a system may not be sustainable.

Although provinces such as British Columbia have argued strongly for the restoration of the funding for PSE cut under the CHST, it appears that this view may not be universally shared. Indeed, one can detect a tacit collusion of sorts between Ottawa and at least certain provinces such as Ontario on the respective roles of the two levels of government. Ontario, for example, in announcing its new "SuperBuild" PSE infrastructure program, is targeting 75% of the money towards expanding programs in information technology, applied technology, health sciences and general sciences.[23] A high proportion will go to community colleges. Ottawa, in turn, has been increasing expenditures on PSE, not through the CHST but rather under the heading of research and development. Federal granting councils, such as the Canadian Institutes for Health Research (formerly the Medical Research Council), the Natural Sciences and Engineering Research Council and the Social Sciences and Humanities Research Council, represent by far the most significant sources of university research funding in Canada. And their role is expanding with recent innovations such as the Canadian Foundation for Innovation (CFI) and the Canada Research Chairs. The latter program, announced in the 2000 federal budget, provides $900 million for 2,000 research chairs by the year 2004–5.[24] The CFI, in turn, has invested more than $800 million in research infrastructure at Canadian universities since August 1998. Under the matching requirements of the program, where both provinces and the private sector are expected to make contributions, the result has been over $2 billion allocated to universities to improve their research facilities.[25]

The significance of these developments is that Ottawa and the provinces appear, with little or no fanfare, to have agreed on a PSE strategy whereby science and technology will be emphasized with Ottawa concentrating on high-end research and postgraduate studies,

---

23. "ON ONTARIO: Century of starvation ahead for liberal arts under Tory plan," *Globe and Mail*, February 28, 2000.

24. The new program is managed by a steering committee composed of the president of the Canada Foundation for Innovation, the deputy minister of Industry Canada and the presidents of the three research-granting agencies. See *Canada Research Chairs: Program Guide* (Ottawa: Tri-Council and CFI Secretariat, 2000).

25. "CFI announces $363 million to boost research capacity at Canadian research institutions," News Release (Ottawa: Canadian Foundation for Innovation, July 26, 2000).

particularly in the medical, engineering and scientific fields. The provinces have said relatively little, if anything, about the desirability of this development. They have, however, with
little protest provided funding to provincial PSE institutions to meet the matching requirements of the CFI program. Even Quebec, the province that back in the 1950s under Premier
Maurice Duplessis prevented universities from receiving direct funding from Ottawa, has
willingly obliged.

The implications of these developments are in some ways quite profound. To the extent
that Ottawa is increasingly channelling new money for PSE through programs such as the
CFI and the Canada Research Chairs, allocations will tend to favour better-off provinces
with the wherewithal to provide matching funding, and the larger PSE institutions within
those provinces, institutions that are best positioned to attract new scholars and private sector funding. The result over time will be a two-tier system of sorts, with the division being
between high-powered, full-service research universities such as the University of Toronto,
the University of British Columbia and McGill on the one hand and smaller liberal arts institutions on the other. There is also a regional division, in that PSE institutions in the have-
not provinces, especially in the Atlantic region, are less well equipped to compete for this
new federal funding. This may be good or bad, depending upon one's perspective. Those
stressing the importance of world-class institutions and the benefits that they can bring to
Canadian society will no doubt favour the two-tier system. Those sympathetic towards
regional balance and the importance of the liberal arts will be disappointed.

To be sure, there is a division of opinion within Ottawa between those in HRDC on the
one hand, who tend to support universal access through mechanisms such as a strengthened
Canada Student Loan program and the CHST, and those in Industry Canada on the other,
who favour the research and development thrust. Given the current position of HRDC,
which is still somewhat under a cloud from the alleged mismanagement of the Transitional
Jobs Fund and at one point facing dismemberment, those factions favouring the research and
development option appear to have the upper hand.

The other point worth noting is that the provinces, knowingly or unknowingly, appear to
be allowing the federal government to provide primary leadership in setting out the role of
the PSE sector with respect to research and development. For example, all universities wish-
ing to participate in the Canada Research Chairs program must submit to Ottawa their
"strategic research plan" outlining objectives and the areas in which the university intends to
deploy the chairs. Since virtually all universities are interested in pursuing one or more of
these chairs (some of the larger institutions stand to receive upwards of 100 chairs), in effect
each university in Canada is *de facto* required to submit to Ottawa a detailed strategic plan.
This plan will be used not only with respect to the Canada Research Chairs but also other
ongoing and future funding programs.

The requirement for a strategic plan is not the first or only condition that Ottawa has
imposed on universities in recent years. Universities are expected to meet employment equity targets under the federal contractors program, for example. As well, a complicated scheme
for ensuring that ethical requirements in federally supported research projects are met has
been recently developed and implemented by the three federal granting councils. These
activities have an impact beyond simply university-based research. For example, holders of
the Canada Research Chairs are expected to spend approximately half their time teaching,
so federal objectives with respect to these chairs will also affect what is taught in classrooms.
In brief, with relatively little debate or protest, Ottawa has carved out a substantial role.
While it may be going too far to say that Ottawa is taking primary responsibility for the future
direction of PSE, it nonetheless appears to have taken an increasingly important role in this
respect.

Conclusion

Developments appear to have come full circle. By the mid-1970s it appeared that Ottawa was quite willing to reduce its role in supporting and developing the PSE sector, preferring instead to focus on labour market development issues where it thought it was probably on firmer jurisdictional ground. Until 1995 there was nothing to suggest that this was not the case, apart from provincial objections. Indeed, the cuts under the newly created CHST suggested that Ottawa might be exiting from the PSE field completely, allowing the CHST to become in effect purely a health and welfare transfer program. Then, however, Ottawa, under pressure from Quebec and the other provinces, decided to abandon in good part the labour market development area. At the same time, quietly but surely, it began revamping and increasing transfers to universities under the rubric of research and development.

Given the salience of globalization and the importance of the knowledge economy, these developments were not something that was likely to elicit much protest either from the university community, which generally has always looked to Ottawa for leadership and funding in this area, or industry, which increasingly began to recognize the importance of advanced education, especially in computer and information-based technologies. The provinces too, or at least some of them such as Ontario, began to realize that targetted spending in engineering and applied science was preferable to simply providing existing institutions with more funding. It would be premature to say either that Ottawa is fully committed to this course or that the provinces have accepted it, but the apparent dovetailing of federal and provincial interests and the clear wish of both levels to avoid the thorny and publicly messy problem of dealing with the issue of universal access to PSE suggests that this may well prove to be the case in the next two to three years.

In brief, it appears that Ottawa's role in the PSE sector is not all that different from what it was back in the early 1960s. The vehicles, or bottles, may be somewhat different, but the ineluctable thrust established by Ottawa in the early postwar period, to set the tone and direction of university life, appears to be alive and well. And in this the SUFA does not appear to be a significant restraint. It may even be irrelevant.

CHAPTER SEVEN

Ready or Not? Hide-and-Seek Politics of Canadian Federalism, the Social Union Framework Agreement, and the Role of National Aboriginal Political Organizations

Michael J. Prince

This chapter focuses on key events leading up to the negotiations and signing of the Social Union Framework Agreement (SUFA), together with intergovernmental processes used since then in its implementation. Process and substance are, of course, closely connected in practice. Process is pivotal to shaping democratic politics and effective policy making, as well as to supporting capacity building and legitimate governance by all governments.

Process refers to organizational structures, and associated participants and nonparticipants, each with certain expectations and value stances, and the patterns of interactions among these actors and ideas in a given context over time. The structures I consider are the federal, provincial and territorial governments plus five national Aboriginal organizations (NAOs). These organizations are the Assembly of First Nations (AFN), Congress of Aboriginal Peoples (CAP), Inuit Tapirisat of Canada (ITC), the Metis National Council (MNC), and the Native Women's Association of Canada (NWAC).

Over the past forty years in Canada, there has been a wave of political organization of Aboriginal activity at the national level and at regional, provincial and local levels. In addition, numerous Aboriginal cultural, economic and social organizations have been created. Along with the growing political organization has been a process of differentiation with new organizations emerging from earlier ones, reflecting the diversities in needs and interests by gender, location, language and history. Today the Aboriginal movement contains a dense network of organizations. The five national organizations considered here are among the prinicpal political agencies for Aboriginal peoples in Canada (see Figure 1).

This chapter addresses five kinds of questions:

> • What role did national Aboriginal leaders and their organizations seek, and what role did they actually play, in events leading to the SUFA?

> • Why was the national Aboriginal leadership excluded from participating in negotiating and securing agreement on the SUFA? What reasons did provincial and federal government leaders give for this exclusion?

> • Since the formulation of the SUFA in February 1999, what has been the experience of the NAOs, in the context of intergovernmental relations, in implementing it?

Figure 1. National Aboriginal Political Organizations

Organization	Origin	Purpose and Scope	Current Leader
Assembly of First Nations (AFN)	Originated as National Indian Council in 1961, called National Indian Brotherhood from 1968-1982	Represents views of over 630 First Nations communities on Aboriginal and treaty rights, economic and social development	Matthew Coon Come, National Chief
Congress of Aboriginal Peoples (CAP)	Formed in 1971, initially called the Native Council of Canada	To serve the interests of Aboriginal peoples living off-reserve across Canada	Harry Daniels, President
Inuit Tapirisat of Canada (ITC)	Created in 1971	Represents views of over 50 Inuit communities in the Northwest Territories, Nunavut, Northern Quebec and Labrador	Okalik Eegeesiak, President
Metis National Council (MNC)	Established in 1983 out of CAP	Acts for Metis people in Canada[1]	Gerald Morin, President
Native Women's Association of Canada (NWAC)	Incorporated in 1974	Promotes the social, economic, cultural and political wellbeing of Status and Non-Status Indian and Metis women across Canada[2]	Presidency vacant

• What contributions are NAOs now making to the social union process and, in turn, how is the process influencing the NAOs and wider Aboriginal movement in Canada?

• Looking ahead, what issues of process face Aboriginal national leaders and the federal, provincial and territorial governments in renewing social policy along with renewing the relationship between Aboriginal and non-Aboriginal peoples?

Not only a framework, the social union is also a frame of mind; it is a way of thinking and feeling about social policy, intergovernmental relations and, more deeply yet, the nature and future of Canada as a political community and diverse society. As a politically negotiated document, the SUFA can be seen in many different ways. For provinces and territories, it is a vehicle for taming federal unilateralism in cutting social-transfer payments and a tool for establishing rules and procedures for the resolution of disputes between governments. For Ottawa, it is an instrument for emphasizing pan-Canadian values and programs, such as the mobility of Canadians, and for legitimating the role of the federal spending power. For governments at all levels, it is an administrative device for modernizing federalism on a more co-operative basis. For at least some social policy groups, it may be a welcome means for restoring much-needed social programs and enabling input in reviewing progress.

For Aboriginal peoples, and other citizens, as individuals at the level of local communities or urban settings, the SUFA is likely widely unknown. For NAOs and their leaders, the SUFA process prompted political mobilization that resulted in a frustrating experience of exclusion. The implementation process, however, is offering in intergovernmental mechanisms the direct representation of Aboriginal interests, values and rights.

---

1. In 1992 the Metis National Council of Women was established as a separate organization.

2. The NWAC initially represented the interests of Inuit women until the formation in 1984 of Pauktuutit, the Inuit Women's Association.

The negotiation process of the SUFA, now the implementation phase, and soon the review stage are all sites that have or will meet with demands for participation by NAOs. The full realization of Aboriginal self-government requires significant revisions to intergovernmental relations and the SUFA is one example of this struggle for self-determination and the recognition of Aboriginal peoples' unique constitutional status in Canadian federalism.

The question is, are we ready or not? Are federal and provincial governments ready to clarify their respective responsibilities to Aboriginal peoples wherever they live in the country? Are we ready to include Aboriginal national leaders in the social-policy renewal process as full and equal partners? Are the NAOs ready to do so? As a country are we ready to implement the philosophy of the Royal Commission on Aboriginal Peoples? If not, we will play a frustrating and reckless game of hide-and-seek politics, in which Aboriginal leaders' claims for involvement and voice in Canadian federalism are obscured or set aside by government elites.

The rest of the chapter is organized as follows: the next section reflects on the interrelationship between recent developments on national unity, the SUFA and executive federalism on the one hand, and Aboriginal national representation on the other. The third section explores why government leaders rejected the inclusion of Aboriginal leaders in the negotiation process of the SUFA. The fourth section outlines the implementation process of the SUFA, and the fifth section ponders whether we are achieving constitutional change by other means. The final section identifies some challenges and questions that we need to reflect on and work on together.

The Road to the Social Union Framework Agreement:
National Unity and Executive Federalism versus Aboriginal Representation

In recent processes to renew the federation and reform the social union, Aboriginal issues and Aboriginal peoples have generally been marginal, despite the efforts of Aboriginal leaders to gain a place within these structures of executive federalism. Consider, for example, the 1997 Calgary Framework for Discussion on National Unity. Triggered by the 1995 federal cuts to health and social-transfer payments and the results of the 1995 Quebec referendum, the premiers undertook to articulate a vision of Canada's values and social programs. The Calgary Framework was such a declaration drafted and agreed to by the premiers (except for Quebec) and territorial leaders in September 1997. The declaration was presented not as a deal among the governments but rather as an expression of ideas and principles for keeping Canada together and as a basis for any future constitutional discussions. These principles are shown in Figure 2.

The Calgary Declaration was an initiative led by the premiers that sought to reach out to the people of Quebec within the context of a broader expression of Canadian values and goals. The intent also was to draft a declaration that was unburdened with other interests seeking constitutional reform.

Aboriginal leaders understandably reacted with dismay over what was both included in the declaration and what was not there. At a meeting in Winnipeg in November 1997, national Aboriginal leaders presented to the premiers and territorial leaders a consensus statement of the five participating NAOs. Their consensus statement outlined a framework of principles, listed below in Figure 3, for a discussion of relationships between federal, provincial and territorial governments and Aboriginal governments and peoples.

The premiers and territorial leaders agreed to receive and consider the Winnipeg statement. They also joined with the Aboriginal leaders in calling on the federal government to recognize their treaty, constitutional and fiduciary obligations towards Aboriginal people, to

Figure 2. The Seven Principles of the Calgary Framework for Discussion on National Unity

---

1. All Canadians are equal and have rights protected by law.
2. All provinces, while diverse in their characteristics, have equality of status.
3. Canada is graced by diversity, tolerance, compassion and an equality of opportunity that is without rival in the world.
4. Canada's gift of diversity includes Aboriginal people and cultures, the vitality of English and French languages, and a multicultural citizenry drawn from all parts of the world.
5. In Canada's federal system, where respect for diversity and equality under lines unity, the unique character of Quebec society, including its French-speaking majority, its culture and its tradition of civil law, is fundamental to the wellbeing of Canada. Consequently, the legislature and Government of Quebec have a role to protect and develop the unique character of Quebec society within Canada.
6. If any future constitutional amendments confer powers on one province, these powers must be available to all provinces.
7. Canada is a federal system where the federal, provincial and territorial governments work in partnership while respecting each other's jurisdictions. Canadians want their governments to work co-operatively and with flexibility to ensure the efficiency and effectiveness of the federation. Canadians want their governments to work together particularly in the delivery of social programs. Provinces and territories renew their commitment to work in partnership with the government of Canada to best serve the needs of Canadians.

Figure 3. The Winnipeg Consensus Statement by National Aboriginal Organizations: A Framework for Discussion on Relationships between Federal, Provincial and Territorial Governments and Aboriginal Governments and Peoples

---

1. The Government of Canada has the historic and primary fiduciary responsibility to all Aboriginal peoples as evidenced by Constitutional, Treaty and Aboriginal rights.
2. The Aboriginal peoples of Canada have, and enjoy, the inherent right of self-government, a right recognized in Section 35 of the Canadian Constitution and in agreements between the federal government and institutions and governments of the Aboriginal peoples and in tripartite and other agreements amongst federal, provincial, territorial and Aboriginal governments and peoples.
3. Provincial, territorial, and federal governments and Aboriginal governments and peoples should seek to work together to resolve issues of resource sharing and management in a manner which will promote economic and social development with certainty and public acceptance without extinguishing or diminishing Aboriginal rights, Treaty rights and Aboriginal title.
4. The re-balancing of Canadian federalism must always be undertaken and accomplished in a manner which does not derogate from the Aboriginal and Treaty rights and jurisdictions of the Aboriginal peoples of Canada. It also must not diminish, in any way, the fiduciary and constitutional responsibilities of Canada and its capacity to honour its commitments and obligations to all Canadians, including the Aboriginal peoples. There must be a willingness to enter into partnerships rejecting federal off-loading to the provinces and to Aboriginal governments and peoples in favour, rather, of joint efforts to maximize best possible uses of available resources.
5. Canada is a federal system in which federal, provincial, and territorial governments and Aboriginal governments and peoples work in partnership while respecting each other's jurisdictions, rights and responsibilities. Nothing in the Calgary communiqué can minimize or derogate from that principle or from existing Aboriginal and Treaty rights.
6. References in the Calgary communiqué to Aboriginal peoples and cultures as one part of Canada's "gift of diversity" must not negate the uniqueness of the place of Aboriginal peoples in Canada, a relationship which finds affirmation in the Treaties and Part II of the Canadian Constitution.
7. The Aboriginal peoples of Canada, the first peoples to govern this land, enjoy their own status and rights, including the equality of Aboriginal men and women, and have the right to ensure the integrity of their societies and to strengthen their relationships with their lands. The role of Aboriginal peoples in the protection and development of their languages, cultures and identities is recognized and supported by Canadians.
8. All governments must be committed to promoting and strengthening identifiable social, political and economic developments which will lead to improved education, housing and infrastructure and to stronger and healthier Aboriginal communities and people, particularly the young and those with special needs.

acknowledge its responsibility to provide programs and services for all Aboriginal people and to end its policies of off-loading these responsibilities to other orders of government. These are not difficult words for provincial and territorial leaders to support since they basically say that Ottawa should assume most if not all the spending responsibilities associated with Aboriginal peoples across Canada. In contrast, the long-standing federal position is that it has primary but not exclusive responsibility for First Nations on reserve and Aboriginal peoples north of 60 degrees, and that the provinces have primary, but not exclusive, responsibility for off-reserve Aboriginal peoples. Without any real compromise on these policy stances by both the federal and provincial orders, the ability to build sustainable Aboriginal communities, particularly in urban areas, will be seriously frustrated.

According to then Saskatchewan premier Roy Romanow, the national Aboriginal leaders

> suggested ways to improve the Calgary Declaration. At the same time, they made it very clear to us that they supported the Declaration's "open hand" to Quebec and are anxious that the premiers' initiative succeed. Their contribution was so constructive that I have sometimes taken to calling our consultation document the Calgary-Winnipeg Declaration.[3]

The premiers and territorial leaders also acknowledged that in any future constitutional review process affecting Aboriginal rights and interests, they will support the participation as equal partners of the five NAOs. Tellingly, no similar commitment was made with respect to the social policy renewal process playing out in the country at the time. This was apparent in December 1997, when the first ministers (with the exception of the premier of Quebec) agreed to mandate their lead social policy ministers to commence negotiations on a framework agreement for Canada's social union that would apply to federal, provincial and territorial governments.

In May 1998, in Quebec City, the five NAOs held an Aboriginal Summit, prior to meeting with federal, provincial and territorial Aboriginal Affairs ministers, the first such meeting with these ministers in four years. The five Aboriginal leaders released another consensus document. In part, the Quebec statement reaffirmed the principles of the Winnipeg declaration. In part, it commented favourably on the recommendations of the Royal Commission on Aboriginal Peoples; and, in part, it argued for inclusive Aboriginal participation at all levels in changes to the social policy renewal process including seats on the federal/provincial/territorial Ministerial Council on Social Policy Renewal.[4] Again, this claim was not adopted.

In early February 1999, days before the first ministers agreed to the SUFA, the then national chief of the Assembly of First Nations, Phil Fontaine, wrote to the prime minister calling on the federal government to directly include First Nations peoples in the social union talks. Fontaine's letter is interesting because it advances a series of arguments for Aboriginal inclusion in the social policy renewal process specifically and intergovernmental relations more generally. The letter is a first-rate example of the argumentative turn of policy analysis and the expressive side of politics. In his open letter, Chief Fontaine put forward six main arguments:

> 1. "Sections 35 and 91 (24) of the Constitution of Canada, Treaty provisions between First Nations and Canada and constitutional and administrative — precedent require our inclusion in this process of restructuring and rebalancing the intergovernmental relationships of the federation." More broadly expressed, Aboriginal

---

3. The Hon. Roy Romanow, "Notes for Remarks," *Canada Seminar at Harvard University* (Boston: Harvard University, February 23, 1998), 13.

4. Aboriginal Summit, "Statement of the Aboriginal Summit" (Quebec City, May 19, 1998).

self-determination and the inherent right to govern includes forging a new part-nership and relationship in federal-provincial-territorial-Aboriginal relations, and this requires the full and equal involvement of national Aboriginal organizations in the Social Union process.

2. The consequences of the Social Union will have direct impacts on Aboriginal peoples and "the nature and quality of social programs available" to them. "Only Aboriginal peoples, not other governments, can properly identify when their needs and interests are affected, and which mechanisms are appropriate to care for those interests." The NAOs, therefore, need to be present and engaged in the talks to identify, anticipate and plan for these impacts *before* any agreement is reached and implemented.

3. The prime minister and the premiers expressed shared agreement among the fed-eral, provincial and territorial governments and Aboriginal organizations at the Quebec City meetings the year before, that "the needs of and resources for Aboriginal peoples are considered in appropriate future federal-provincial-territorial agreements or arrangements."

4. National Aboriginal leaders need to be at the talks in order to ensure that the interests and rights of Aboriginal peoples are not derogated or diminished in any way by any new intergovernmental arrangements.

5. Beyond concerns of protecting rights, Aboriginal leaders have a unique and pos-itive contribution to make to new intergovernmental arrangements and to the review and renewal of Canada's social programs.

6. Other processes in which First Nations and other Aboriginal organizations are involved with the federal and provincial/territorial governments do not, and can not, address the implications for Aboriginal peoples contained in the Social Union and Health Accord negotiations. Inclusion in the Social Union talks must be a crit-ical supplement to the involvement of Aboriginal national leaders in other meet-ings of First Ministers, cabinet ministers and officials on issues fundamental to the interests of Aboriginal peoples.[5]

This case for direct Aboriginal representation in the social union talks rests on a sophis-ticated and interrelated set of constitutional, empirical and normative forms of reasoning. The vision of Canadian federalism underpinning the arguments is, to quote again from Fontaine's letter, a "system in which federal, provincial, territorial and Aboriginal govern-ments and peoples strive to work together in partnerships while respecting each others' juris-dictions, rights and responsibilities." The social union talks were viewed as a "historic process of nation building" that affects Aboriginal peoples, their governments and their place within the federation. Yet leaders from NAOs were not direct parties to the social union or the health accord negotiations that took place in 1999 and in 2000.

Left Out Again: Why Were Aboriginal Leaders Excluded?

Some months before the SUFA was reached, Keith Banting noted that

the greatest danger facing the social union is that the current negotiations will be driven exclusively by those hardy perennials of Canadian politics, namely, money and power. *The danger is that the debate will proceed completely within the intellectual framework of federalism*, focusing only on issues such as fiscal imbalance, federal-

---

5. National Chief Phil Fontaine, "Letter to the Prime Minister" (Ottawa, February 2, 1999).

provincial transfers, visibility, accountability, mechanisms to increase intergovern-mental cooperation, and the like.[6]

Certainly these issues of federalism are of fundamental importance, but need to be balanced, Banting argued, with values concerning the substance of social policy and visions of our mul-tiple identities and communities. However, claims for Aboriginal representation in the social union process lay outside the dominant framework of federalism and the challenges of national unity as defined by federal and provincial political elites. From their vantage points, the pressing issues were the need to respond to the trials of the February 1995 federal budg-et cuts in transfers and the razor-close results of the October 1995 Quebec referendum. Against these immediate events was a general public tired of intergovernmental squabbling, and increasingly worried about the sustainability of health care and the affordability of post-secondary education.

The response by provinces and territories was guided by the habits of executive federal-ism as expressed by the formation of the Ministerial Council on Social Policy Renewal, then the Calgary Declaration, and then social union negotiations with the federal government through 1998 and into 1999. The social union process can be seen as one initiated by the premiers in 1995 to engage the federal government in a new partnership in the areas of pri-marily provincial jurisdiction — health care, education, social services and social assistance — with new money and new rules for managing their relationship.

It is hard to escape the impression that Aboriginal affairs was treated as a separate file, as a policy sector not directly applicable to the task at hand for first ministers. A case of feder-al-provincial summitry, the social union negotiations were about managing disagreements and affirming certain shared constitutional and policy norms at the level of central officials and executive politicians. Reasons given by leaders for the exclusion of Aboriginal national leaders are that "the talks were not a constitutional proposal, but merely an administrative arrangement" and that "delivery of social programs continues to be a provincial responsi-bility."[7] Moreover, leaders pointed to two statements in the actual SUFA that specifically spoke of Aboriginal peoples. The first section on principles says, in language reflective of the Winnipeg Consensus Statement and Fontaine's letter, that "for greater clarity, nothing in this agreement abrogates or derogates from any Aboriginal treaty or other rights of Aboriginal peoples including self-government." Indeed, this language is very similar to section 25 of the Charter of Rights and Freedoms in the Constitution Act, 1982. In section 4 on "working in partnership for Canadians," it states that "government will work with Aboriginal peoples of Canada to find practical solutions to address their pressing needs."

The first statement is meant as a symbolic reassurance to the Aboriginal national leaders, absent from the process, that the rights of Aboriginal peoples are not cancelled or weakened by the agreement. Federal and provincial/territorial governments commit to this principle "within their respective constitutional jurisdictions and powers." The problem is, however, that the meaning of these rights in practical terms is the subject of jurisdictional dispute between the federal and provincial orders. Unlike the other sectors discussed in the SUFA, which have involved Ottawa giving the provinces new or more stable funding and/or more authority over the management of programs (for example, labour market programs and social housing administration), provinces are not seeking more powers or responsibilities for Aboriginal affairs.

---

6. Keith G. Banting, "Social Citizenship and the Social Union in Canada," *Policy Options-Options politiques* 19, no. 9 (November 1998): 33. Emphasis added.

7. CBC News, "Premiers and aboriginal leaders meet," February 11, 1999, and "Native leaders want a place at table with premiers," March 21, 1999.

The second statement pledges governments to work with Aboriginal peoples on "their pressing needs." Given the exclusion of Aboriginal representatives from negotiating the social union, this laudatory statement rings with contradiction. There is no indication that the problems of Aboriginal peoples are Canadian problems, nor mention of Aboriginal nations, governments or national political organizations. The reference to finding practical solutions suggests that the high politics of treaty negotiations, constitutional reform efforts and judicial actions are not what is being implied here. Nowhere else in the SUFA are Aboriginal peoples mentioned. They are absent from the section on the federal spending power, the section on dispute avoidance and resolution, and the section on the review of the SUFA. Perhaps it is a case of out of sight, out of mind.

These deficiencies are striking in light of the Royal Commission on Aboriginal Peoples five-volume final report having been released in the midst of this context.[8] Throughout the Royal Commission's volumes is the theme that the NAOs are important partners in working in close consultation with federal, provincial and territorial governments based on the principles of mutual recognition, mutual respect, and mutual responsibility. The commissioners saw NAOs as working with Aboriginal communities, nations and other Aboriginal organizations to formulate and implement health, education, training, and social services programs. On behalf of the Aboriginal peoples of Canada, NAOs were regarded as central means of expression for building a renewed relationship. Formulating the SUFA within the executive federalism of Ottawa, the provinces and the territories, without the involvement of national Aboriginal leaders, was a rebuff to this part of the Royal Commission's vision for governance. While these deficiencies are striking, they are not altogether surprising given that neither the federal government nor the provinces fully embraced the Royal Commission reports, in effect placing the concerns of the NAOs as footnotes in the SUFA.

Implementing the SUFA: NAOs Are Finding a Role

Putting the SUFA into practice is of great interest because, so far, the implementation process has not been as discouraging and exclusionary for Aboriginal organizations as was the negotiation phase. The SUFA sets out guidelines for governments to follow in developing and implementing new social programs; it does not prescribe what programs should be undertaken, nor does it set out social policy priorities. While national Aboriginal leaders lost out in the adoption stage of the social union, there are some new and enhanced opportunities for participation by NAOs in carrying out the SUFA.

Instigating the SUFA is not a simple top-down process but rather an example of adaptive implementation in which the initial agreement is adapting to, and being defined in more concrete terms by, the goals and interests of the various participants engaged in renewing social programs. The process can be viewed as an expanded form of executive federalism: incorporating Aboriginal participation as represented by the five NAOs, with additional bargaining taking place. Having more participants and goals involved may make implementation of the SUFA more complicated, but it will produce a more inclusive, more responsive and probably more legitimate process and set of policy outcomes.

Just a week after the SUFA was signed, Premier Romanow, as the then chair of the annual premiers' conference, issued an invitation to the five national Aboriginal leaders to meet with premiers and territorial leaders. According to Romanow, the purpose of the meeting was to allow the Aboriginal leaders "to have their say about social programs as they affect

---

8. Canada, *Report of the Royal Commission on Aboriginal Peoples* (Ottawa: Supply and Service Canada, 1996).

them."[9] More than that, Aboriginal leaders wanted to impress upon federal and provincial leaders the requirement to consult with national Aboriginal organizations and to treat them as equals.

A one-day meeting took place in March 1999, in Regina, between the leaders of the five NAOs, with six premiers and two territorial leaders in attendance. The six premiers there represented the provinces of British Columbia, Alberta, Saskatchewan, Manitoba, Ontario, and Nova Scotia. The federal government was not invited to this meeting. The meeting's agenda included the issues of the SUFA itself, an Aboriginal youth strategy, and social problems for Aboriginal peoples living in urban centres of Canada. Provincial and territorial leaders expressed support for the involvement of the NAOs in the implementation of the SUFA "wherever such implementation has implications for Aboriginal people." The premiers and representatives of the five NAOs issued a call for the prime minister to hold a first ministers and aboriginal leaders meeting to discuss the Royal Commission's recommendations and, by implication, the federal government's action plan on Aboriginal policy, Gathering Strength.

Fontaine was pleased with the result of the meeting, saying: "We came here to secure a commitment from the premiers to have Aboriginal people fully integrated in the process of the further development of the Social Union Framework Agreement. I believe we have that commitment." Premiers and territorial leaders did not, however, endorse a proposal by National Chief Fontaine that a companion agreement be created to the SUFA, a parallel accord giving Aboriginal organizations a formal role in any future negotiations between the federal and provincial and territorial governments. Such a companion accord went too far for the premiers and, in any event, would require consent of the federal government and presumably the other provinces absent from the March 1999 meeting. While there was not a specific reference to a companion accord, Fontaine nonetheless claimed "it is understood that the commitment to engage our people in all future discussions and processes related to the Social Union Framework Agreement is in reference to the companion accord."[10]

Romanow seemed to echo this view in remarks after the meeting, commenting that, "I think we have found common ground. The common ground is our willingness to establish a mechanism where the voice of Aboriginal leaders about their concerns is heard loudly and clearly."[11]

Aboriginal organizations are participating in intergovernmental relations on three fronts: (1) bilaterally with the federal government; (2) bilaterally and multilaterally with the provincial and territorial governments; and (3) with the federal and provincial-territorial governments simultaneously. In all cases, these relations occur between political executives and/or senior public servants. In relation to the SUFA, formal intergovernmental mechanisms in which the NAOs are participating include:

> 1. The "dialogue process" for the new National Children's Agenda announced in May 1999, along with a discussion paper, *A National Children's Agenda: Developing a Shared Vision* and a supplementary paper, *Measuring Child Wellbeing and Monitoring Progress*. Both papers resulted from general consultations among, and input from, federal, provincial and territorial governments and the NAOs. The *Shared Vision* document states, "There are compelling reasons for Aboriginal people to participate as more than half of the Aboriginal population is made up of children, a trend counter to Canadian demographics."[12] In announcing the release of these papers,

9. CBC News, "First Nations air social union beefs," March 22, 1999.

10. Canadian Press, "Premiers back Aboriginals over stake in social union," March 23, 1999.

11. CBC News, "Aboriginal leaders will have say on social union," March 23, 1999.

12. Federal-Provincial-Territorial Council on Social Policy Renewal, "Federal, Provincial and Territorial Governments Launch Dialogue Process for National Children's Agenda," 2 (News Release, May 7, 1999).

the lead federal minister stated in his address that the National Children's Agenda "is a unique opportunity to work closely with Aboriginal Canadians to address the needs of Aboriginal children." "Special efforts," the federal minister declared, "are also going to be made to have Aboriginal participation." Harry Daniels, president of CAP, underscored this at the announcement. "We have to be involved in every step of the process in developing some kind of strategy that is going to see our kids wind up with something that's concrete for them. The monitoring progress is certainly going to be high on our agenda ... because we want to see this succeed."[13]

2. Federal/provincial/territorial (FPT) working groups of officials, consisting of representatives from the five NAOs, are being assembled as of early 2000 to work on social policy issues that relate to Aboriginal peoples.

3. The first ever meeting of the FPT Ministerial Council on Social Policy Renewal, ministers responsible for Aboriginal Affairs, and the five NAO leaders was held in December 1999. This group has agreed to meet again within a year.

4. The FPT Ministerial Council on Social Policy Renewal Co-Chairs and the national Aboriginal leaders last met in February 1997, but have now agreed to meet again by mid-2000 to review the outcomes of the working group.

Other significant and recent intergovernmental mechanisms that include Aboriginal officials and bear on social policy, though not specifically tied to the SUFA, contain:

1. the five-year national accords for Human Resources Development Agreements signed between Human Resources Development Canada and each of the five NAOs over the February–April 1999 period[14];

2. the meeting of senior Aboriginal representatives and FPT deputy ministers responsible for Aboriginal Affairs in November 1999; and

3. the meeting, in December 1999, of FPT ministers responsible for Aboriginal Affairs and the NAO leaders from which came agreement to meet at least once a year.

National Aboriginal leaders, and their representatives, are starting to get to the table or, more precisely, a number of intergovernmental relations tables. This is reminiscent of the experience of the territories in their evolution through the 1970s and 1980s toward responsible government.[15] For Aboriginal peoples there is an elaboration of mechanisms with multiple locales at the political level for interaction between the NAOs and governments, and some as well at the administrative level. The number of intergovernmental meetings with direct Aboriginal participation has been growing, from hardly any such conferences, just a few years ago, to now several each year at political and administrative levels.[16]

Achieving Constitutional Change by Other Means?

The SUFA exists within the larger political union, the federal system, which itself is in transition. Alan Cairns has made the argument that "with the exception of Northwest

---

13. Canadian Press, "Ministers announce new children's agenda," May 8, 1999.

14. For details on these agreements see the web site: http://HRDC-DRHC.GC.CA/common/ news/dept http://www.HRDC-DRHC.GC.CA/common/news/dept. The relevant news releases are 99–12, 99–18, 99–36, and 99–41.

15. Michael J. Prince and Gary Juniper, *Public Power and the Public Purse: Governments, Budgets, and Aboriginal Peoples in the Canadian North* (Ottawa: Royal Commission on Aboriginal Peoples, 1995).

16. Based on information of meetings reported by the Canadian Intergovernmental Conference Secretariat web site: http://www.scics.gc.ca/cinfo. Not all meetings are reported here.

Figure 4. Expressed Principles and Emergent Practices on the Place of National Aboriginal Organizations within Intergovernmental Relations

---

1. Federal, provincial and territorial governments will work with the Aboriginal peoples of Canada to find practical solutions to address their pressing social policy needs.
2. While Quebec did not sign the Social Union Framework Agreement, the Quebec governmen t has expressed its willingness to work with Aboriginal representatives to improve the situation of Aboriginal people in the spirit of its own Aboriginal Affairs guidelines.
3. National Aboriginal Organizations will be engaged in the implementation and review of the Social Union Framework Agreement wherever such activities have implications for Aboriginal peoples.
4. National Aboriginal leaders are to meet with federal -provincial-territorial ministers responsible for Aboriginal Affairs as well as the Ministerial Council on Social Policy Renewal.
5. Resources for the National Aboriginal Organizations to participate fully in working groups set up on SUFA will be negotiated with the federal government and the organizations.
6. These processes will not replace existing mech anisms for Aboriginal involvement in various initiatives underway, nor preclude participation in other national or regional initiatives.
7. Nothing in such mechanisms and processes abrogates or derogates from any Aboriginal treaty or other rights of Aboriginal peoples, including self-government.

Sources: *A Framework to Improve the Social Union for Canadians* (Ottawa: February 4, 1999), Meeting of Premiers/Territorial Leaders and Leaders of National Aboriginal Organizations, *News Release* (Regina: March 22, 1999), and Meeting of the Federal-Provincial-Territorial Ministerial Council on Social Policy Renewal, Ministers Responsible for Aboriginal Matters and Leaders of National Aboriginal Organizations, *News Release* (Ottawa: December 16, 1999).

Territories," and now Nunavut, federalism "is more an unsympathetic container for the sympathetic expression of Aboriginal realties." Consequently, Cairns thinks that the adaptation of Canadian federalism "will almost certainly require an entrenched third order of Aboriginal government."[17] If Cairns' assessment is correct, and there is much to support it in both our distant and recent history (Johnston, 1993; Cairns, 2000), his solution raises the dim prospects of formal megaconstitutional reform. Such reform is a most unlikely story line in view of the contemporary politics of national unity and our present national leadership.

What the SUFA and implementation process offer is another avenue for strengthening the role of Aboriginal political organizations within Canada's network of intergovernmental relations, in other words, government-to-government-to-government working relationships. It is quite true that the SUFA is only a three-year administrative agreement, not an entrenched constitutional amendment; however, there is, I would argue, no going back. The SUFA, the Regina communiqué of March 1999, and subsequent implementation mechanisms point to constitutional change by other, developmental means for the place of Aboriginal peoples within Canadian federalism (see Figure 4).

The SUFA and official news releases reporting decisions from intergovernmental meetings over the past year are giving formal administrative and written recognition to the role of NAOs in the conduct of Canadian federalism. These expressed principles and emergent practices are just that; they are nonjusticiable commitments (that is, public pledges with no legal status and thus nonenforceable in the courts) for guiding intergovernmental conduct. They are modest measures for modernizing and democratizing how governments should interact with Aboriginal organizations and leaders in the social union process and in federalism more generally. Nonetheless, the measures should help make federalism more a "sympathetic expression of aboriginal realities." If routinely observed over time, these practices

---

17. Alan Cairns, "The Fragmentation of Canadian Citizenship," in William Kaplan (ed.), *The Meaning and Future of Canadian Citizenship* (Montreal and Kingston: McGill-Queen's University Press, 1993), 187. See also Alan C. Cairns, *Citizens Plus: Aboriginal Peoples and the Canadian State* (Vancouver: University of British Columbia Press, 2000).

possibly will crystallize into conventions of responsible federalism, customs having a degree of political if not moral obligation to respect by governments.[18]

Despite being excluded from the negotiation of the SUFA, NAOs are having an effect on the social union in the implementation stage. Aboriginal groups are questioning and altering somewhat successfully the theory and practice of executive federalism. NAOs are making the social policy renewal process more inclusive by securing recognition of claims for direct representation and participation in certain intergovernmental structures. As a result, Aboriginal groups are helping to frame the meaning of the social union, thereby enhancing the legitimacy of social policy initiatives such as the National Children's Agenda and raising the salience of Aboriginal perspectives and priorities at the Canada-wide level.

In turn, the social union process is itself having an influence on the NAOs and wider Aboriginal political movement in Canada. It is by recognizing once again in Canadian politics and policy the collective identity of Aboriginal peoples, an identity that has a network of formal organizations with shared values and similar goals. It is by presenting specific structures as the spaces for inclusion in policy development, program delivery and evaluation. And it is by setting boundaries as to which national organizations are the ones to be involved in speaking for Aboriginal peoples in these processes and which are left out. For example, the Native Women's Association of Canada is included but the Metis National Council of Women and the Inuit Women's Association are not.

The hide-and-seek politics of Canadian federalism, therefore, are not over for Aboriginal peoples. National Aboriginal leaders remain excluded from routine participation in the Annual Premiers' Conferences, a political body of growing importance, and from the regionally based Atlantic and Western premiers' conferences. In addition, Aboriginal peoples are frustrated by the prime minister's continued refusal to convene a conference of first ministers and national Aboriginal leaders to discuss the recommendations of the Royal Commission.

Looking Ahead: Some Challenges and Questions

The Social Union process calls attention to a number of thorny issues and questions that we need to think more about and to work on together. Here I briefly refer to four challenges for consideration.

First, our working understanding of intergovernmental relations must make a place for NAOs: they are part of the political system and social policy network, connected to regional and local Aboriginal groups and communities, and interacting with the provinces, municipalities, territories and federal government. The political elite, the mass media, and the political science–public administration academic community all need to more fully recognize that intergovernmental relations embrace federal-Aboriginal, provincial-Aboriginal, territorial-Aboriginal, municipal-Aboriginal, inter-Aboriginal, and federal-provincial-territorial– Aboriginal relationships.

A second challenge relates to wider public participation in intergovernmental relations. The SUFA contains commitments on greater public engagement in the policy process, which raise expectations — if nothing else — in the short term. What would increased public participation in the social policy realm really mean for NAOs? To the extent that there is significant resistance within the public to the political agenda of the NAOs, this could be a serious obstacle to their securing an increasingly more formal role in policy development. One

---

18. Peter W. Hogg, *Constitutional Law of Canada 2000* (Toronto: Carswell, 2000).

response to this possible stumbling block, an approach already in practice, is the formation of bilateral arrangements between a government and one or more NAOs.

A third challenge concerns the age-old and enduring difference between the federal government on the one side and the provinces on the other, regarding the financial responsibilities of each order for meeting the needs and the rights of Aboriginal peoples in Canada. How can this buck passing, the ultimate form of hide-and-seek politics, be resolved? How can we abide by the federal principle of respect for the constitutional division of powers and, at the same time, respect the Aboriginal principle of self-determination and fundamental rights? The inclusion of NAOs within executive federalism would force the question and shift the dynamics toward finding common ground.

A fourth challenge is the complex and at times competitive relationship between Aboriginal organizations, at the national level and between national and regional organizations, in representing certain constituencies of Aboriginal peoples, especially the urban-based population.[19] Which Aboriginal organizations are to be included in intergovernmental meetings? For whom do particular Aboriginal leaders speak? Matthew Coon Come, the national chief of the AFN, has raised precisely this issue for First Nations' peoples. Chief Coon Come has recently written that:

> in Ottawa's policy of the narrowing and extinguishment of our Aboriginal and treaty rights, it has been necessary since 1982 for the federal government to appear to be obtaining our consent. The AFN is constituted as an umbrella organization with a national chief who is, to a significant extent, a figurehead. This historic power imbalance between Aboriginal peoples and the Crown will only change if we think differently about our national organization. Is it just an umbrella organization, or do we want it to be something more, something capable of asserting and defending fundamental rights?[20]

This relates in part the topic of the practice of political representation and the meaning of citizenship in Canada. Is there a problem of "double representation" of the Inuit, for example, if both the ITC and Nunavut government are at the intergovernmental table? A similar question may be posed of the representation of Aboriginal men and women, in relation to the AFN, NWAC and the CAP. A degree of competition among NAOs, as our familiarity with federalism more generally points up, is likely inevitable and frequently a positive force for dialogue and political developments. So we should not use the diversity among NAOs as an excuse for continuing to exclude Aboriginal leaders from the many tables of intergovernmental relations. The idea of annual Aboriginal summits of the NAO leaders might also serve a useful role for the development of shared goals, priorities and positions on policy matters.

Early experience with implementing the SUFA shows that after considerable struggle by Aboriginal groups, some provincial leadership, and federal support, Aboriginal access to the processes of federalism can be achieved. Do we want to democratize further our brand of federalism? If we do, and truly wish to create a new relationship between Aboriginal and non-Aboriginal peoples, then direct participation by Aboriginal national leaders in the negotiation and ratification of future intergovernmental agreements on social policy must be a central feature of twenty-first-century Canada.

---

19. See Frances Abele, Katherine A. Graham and Allan M. Maslove, "Negotiating Canada: Changes in Aboriginal Policy over the Last Thirty Years," in Leslie A. Pal (ed.), *How Ottawa Spends 1999-2000, Shape Shifting: Canadian Governance toward the Twenty-first Century* (Toronto: Oxford University Press, 1999), 251–92; David Roberts, "Premiers agree to mull native role in social-union talks," *Globe and Mail,* March 23, 1999, A4.

20. Matthew Coon Come, "We have a dream, too" *Globe and Mail,* January 31, 2001, A13.

.

A Framework to Improve the Social Union for Canadians

An Agreement Between the Government of Canada and the Governments of the Provinces and Territories

February 4, 1999

The following agreement is based upon a mutual respect between orders of government and a willingness to work more closely together to meet the needs of Canadians.

1. Principles

Canada's social union should reflect and give expression to the fundamental values of Canadians — equality, respect for diversity, fairness, individual dignity and responsibility, and mutual aid and our responsibilities for one another.

Within their respective constitutional jurisdictions and powers, governments commit to the following principles:

All Canadians are equal

· Treat all Canadians with fairness and equity

· Promote equality of opportunity for all Canadians

· Respect the equality, rights and dignity of all Canadian women and men and their diverse needs

Meeting the needs of Canadians

· Ensure access for all Canadians, wherever they live or move in Canada, to essential social programs and services of reasonably comparable quality

· Provide appropriate assistance to those in need

· Respect the principles of medicare: comprehensiveness, universality, portability, public administration and accessibility

· Promote the full and active participation of all Canadians in Canada's social and economic life

· Work in partnership with individuals, families, communities, voluntary organizations, business and labour, and ensure appropriate opportunities for Canadians to have meaningful input into social policies and programs

Sustaining social programs and services

· Ensure adequate, affordable, stable and sustainable funding for social programs

Aboriginal peoples of Canada

· For greater certainty, nothing in this agreement abrogates or derogates from any Aboriginal, treaty or other rights of Aboriginal peoples including self-government

2. Mobility within Canada

All governments believe that the freedom of movement of Canadians to pursue opportunities anywhere in Canada is an essential element of Canadian citizenship.

Governments will ensure that no new barriers to mobility are created in new social policy initiatives.

Governments will eliminate, within three years, any residency-based policies or practices which constrain access to post-secondary education, training, health and social services and social assistance unless they can be demonstrated to be reasonable and consistent with the principles of the Social Union Framework.

Accordingly, sector ministers will submit annual reports to the Ministerial Council identifying residency-based barriers to access and providing action plans to eliminate them.

Governments are also committed to ensure, by July 1, 2001, full compliance with the mobility provisions of the Agreement on Internal Trade by all entities subject to those provisions, including the requirements for mutual recognition of occupational qualifications and for eliminating residency requirements for access to employment opportunities.

3. Informing Canadians — Public Accountability and Transparency

Canada's Social Union can be strengthened by enhancing each government's transparency and accountability to its constituents. Each government therefore agrees to:

Achieving and measuring results

· Monitor and measure outcomes of its social programs and report regularly to its constituents on the performance of these programs

· Share information and best practices to support the development of outcome measures, and work with other governments to develop, over time, comparable indicators to measure progress on agreed objectives

· Publicly recognize and explain the respective roles and contributions of governments

· Use funds transferred from another order of government for the purposes agreed and pass on increases to its residents

· Use third parties, as appropriate, to assist in assessing progress on social priorities

Involvement of Canadians

· Ensure effective mechanisms for Canadians to participate in developing social priorities and reviewing outcomes

Ensuring fair and transparent practices

· Make eligibility criteria and service commitments for social programs publicly available

· Have in place appropriate mechanisms for citizens to appeal unfair administrative practices and bring complaints about access and service

· Report publicly on citizen's appeals and complaints, ensuring that confidentiality requirements are met

4. Working in partnership for Canadians

Joint Planning and Collaboration

The Ministerial Council has demonstrated the benefits of joint planning and mutual help through which governments share knowledge and learn from each other.

Governments therefore agree to

· Undertake joint planning to share information on social trends, problems and priorities and to work together to identify priorities for collaborative action

· Collaborate on implementation of joint priorities when this would result in more effective and efficient service to Canadians, including as appropriate joint development of objectives and principles, clarification of roles and responsibilities, and flexible implementation to respect diverse needs and circumstances, complement existing measures and avoid duplication

Reciprocal Notice and Consultation

The actions of one government or order of government often have significant effects on other governments. In a manner consistent with the principles of our system of parliamentary government and the budget-making process, governments therefore agree to:

· Give one another advance notice prior to implementation of a major change in a social policy or program which will likely substantially affect another government

· Offer to consult prior to implementing new social policies and programs that are likely to substantially affect other governments or the social union more generally. Governments participating in these consultations will have the opportunity to identify potential duplication and to propose alternative approaches to achieve flexible and effective implementation

Equitable Treatment

For any new Canada-wide social initiatives, arrangements made with one province/territory will be made available to all provinces/territories in a manner consistent with their diverse circumstances.

Aboriginal Peoples

Governments will work with the Aboriginal peoples of Canada to find practical solutions to address their pressing needs.

5. The federal spending power — Improving social programs for Canadians

Social transfers to provinces and territories

The use of the federal spending power under the Constitution has been essential to the development of Canada's social union. An important use of the spending power by the Government of Canada has been to transfer money to the provincial and territorial governments. These transfers support the delivery of social programs and services by provinces and territories in order to promote equality of opportunity and mobility for all Canadians and to pursue Canada-wide objectives.

Conditional social transfers have enabled governments to introduce new and innovative social programs, such as Medicare, and to ensure that they are available to all Canadians. When the federal government uses such conditional transfers, whether cost-shared or block-funded, it should proceed in a cooperative manner that is respectful of the provincial and territorial governments and their priorities.

Funding predictability

The Government of Canada will consult with provincial and territorial governments at least one year prior to renewal or significant funding changes in existing social transfers to provinces-territories, unless otherwise agreed, and will build due notice provisions into any new social transfers to provincial-territorial governments.

New Canada-wide initiatives supported by transfers to provinces and territories

With respect to any new Canada-wide initiatives in health care, post-secondary education, social assistance and social services that are funded through intergovernmental transfers, whether block funded or cost shared, the Government of Canada will:

· Work collaboratively with all provincial and territorial governments to identify Canada-wide priorities and objectives

· Not introduce such new initiatives without the agreement of a majority of provincial governments

Each provincial and territorial government will determine the detailed program design and mix best suited to its own needs and circumstances to meet the agreed objectives.

A provincial-territorial government which, because of its existing programming, does not require the total transfer to fulfill the agreed objectives would be able to reinvest any funds not required for those objectives in the same or a related priority area.

The Government of Canada and the provincial-territorial governments will agree on an accountability framework for such new social initiatives and investments.

All provincial and territorial governments that meet or commit to meet the agreed Canada-wide objectives and agree to respect the accountability framework will receive their share of available funding.

Direct federal spending

Another use of the federal spending power is making transfers to individuals and to organizations in order to promote equality of opportunity, mobility, and other Canada-wide objectives.

When the federal government introduces new Canada-wide initiatives funded through direct transfers to individuals or organizations for health care, post-secondary education, social assistance and social services, it will, prior to implementation, give at least three months' notice and offer to consult. Governments participating in these consultations will have the opportunity to identify potential duplication and to propose alternative approaches to achieve flexible and effective implementation.

6. Dispute Avoidance and Resolution

Governments are committed to working collaboratively to avoid and resolve intergovernmental disputes. Respecting existing legislative provisions, mechanisms to avoid and resolve disputes should:

· Be simple, timely, efficient, effective and transparent

· Allow maximum flexibility for governments to resolve disputes in a nonadversarial way

· Ensure that sectors design processes appropriate to their needs

· Provide for appropriate use of third parties for expert assistance and advice while ensuring democratic accountability by elected officials

Dispute avoidance and resolution will apply to commitments on mobility, intergovernmental transfers, interpretation of the Canada Health Act principles, and, as appropriate, on any new joint initiative.

Sector ministers should be guided by the following process, as appropriate:

Dispute avoidance

· Governments are committed to working together and avoiding disputes through information sharing, joint planning, collaboration, advance notice and early consultation, and flexibility in implementation

Sector negotiations

· Sector negotiations to resolve disputes will be based on joint fact finding

· A written joint fact-finding report will be submitted to governments involved, who will have the opportunity to comment on the report before its completion

· Governments involved may seek assistance of a third party for fact finding, advice, or mediation

· At the request of either party in a dispute, fact-finding or mediation reports will be made public

Review provisions

· Any government can require a review of a decision or action one year after it enters into effect or when changing circumstances justify.

Each government involved in a dispute may consult and seek advice from third parties including interested or knowledgeable persons or groups, at all stages of the process.

Governments will report publicly on an annual basis on the nature of intergovernmental disputes and their resolution.

Role of the Ministerial Council

The Ministerial Council will support sector ministers by collecting information on effective ways of implementing the agreement and avoiding disputes and receiving reports from jurisdictions on progress on commitments under the Social Union Framework Agreement.

7. Review of the Social Union Framework Agreement

By the end of the third year of the Framework Agreement, governments will jointly undertake a full review of the Agreement and its implementation and make appropriate adjustments to the Framework as required. This review will ensure significant opportunities for input and feedback from Canadians and all interested parties, including social policy experts, and private-sector and voluntary organizations.